'Perish the Privileged Orders'

Other books on history and politics published by New Clarion Press

'Perish the Privileged Orders'

A socialist history of the Chartist movement

Mark O'Brien

New Clarion Press

1st edition published in 1995 by Redwords
This revised edition published in 2009 by:

New Clarion Press
5 Church Row, Gretton
Cheltenham GL54 5HG
England

New Clarion Press is a workers' co-operative.

A catalogue record for this book is available from the British Library.

ISBN   978 1 873797 52 5

Typeset by Paul Leather, PLGraphics, Coventry
Printed in Great Britain by imprintdigital.net, Upton Pyne, Exeter

Contents

For Eileen McMahon
Socialist: born 1913; died 1998

And for Kate, Rohina and Ruben

Preface

When the first edition of this book was published in 1995, it seemed relevant in many ways to debates within the working-class and trade union movement. Principally I wished to reassert both the struggle that characterised the origins of the British working-class movement as well as the socialist influence within it. In the mid-1990s, before the rise of the major social justice movements of the late 1990s and early 2000s, those who defended the idea that mass action had the power to alter the course of history, let alone do so in a socialist direction, were in an isolated position. The story of the Chartists at that time was an important antidote to the influential idea that the British working-class movement had always been essentially subservient, dominated by a culture of deference and the politics of piecemeal reform.

As the second edition of this book appears, the Chartist movement certainly remains relevant in this broadly historical sense. Its relevance has also changed, however, and in ways that seem deeper and more connected to the numerous fronts on which working-class people find themselves having to fight today. Although our world is very different from that of the Chartists, they would nonetheless have recognised many of its tensions and issues as being similar to those that drove their movement. In an era in which civil liberties, new forms of colonialism, the harassment of minorities and economic injustice have become topics of renewed contention and struggle, the Chartist experience is resonant. Moreover, bitter disappointment with government promises that things would 'only get better' provides the backdrop to popular political anger in Britain today, just as the failure of the Whigs to deliver the working-class vote served to fuel the Chartist movement.

The Chartists are relevant also in one crucial final sense. This was a movement that emerged from the confluence of many campaigns and struggles. Today the many campaigns of working people against the logic of the market in public services, for fair treatment at work, against job losses, against racism in workplaces and communities, and for trade union rights can converge into a movement that may, once again, reach the heights that the Chartists achieved – both in the sense of the challenge it represented to the oppression and corruption of the political establishment, and in terms of the inspiration and courage that carried it forward. It may also, of course, go beyond the Chartists to achieve the social as well as political change that they ultimately yearned for.

Mark O'Brien, Liverpool, September 2009

Chapter 1   The makings of a movement

Workers' lives

> *It was a town of machinery and tall chimneys, out of which interminable serpents of smoke trailed themselves for ever and ever, and never got uncoiled. It had a black canal in it, and a river that ran purple with ill-smelling dye, and vast piles of building full of windows where there was a rattling and a trembling all day long, and where the piston of the steam-engine worked monotonously up and down, like the head of an elephant in a state of melancholy madness.*

Coketown, the setting of Dickens' *Hard Times*, gives us a glimpse of the new towns that were springing up throughout Victorian England in the first half of the nineteenth century. Manchester, Leeds, Bradford, Halifax and others bore witness to the furious pace of urbanisation which the industrial revolution had brought with it. As the new cities sucked in labour from the surrounding areas, they tore up the old rural customs and social relations. Whole populations had been forced off the land by the Enclosure Acts, families had been broken apart and thousands now poured into the urban ghettos every month. It was within these new towns, and the conditions they bred, that the radical movements that converged in Chartism began to grow.

The living conditions that greeted the new migrants into the cities were horrific. Descriptions of the overcrowding, filth and disease beggar belief today. One report from Preston in 1842 stated:

> *The streets, courts and yards examined contain about 422 dwellings inhabited at the time of the enquiry by 2,400 persons sleeping in 852 beds, i.e. an average of 5.68 inhabitants in each house and 2.8 persons to each bed.*[1]

The report showed that it was not uncommon for four or five people to be sleeping together and that in a handful of cases seven or even eight people were sharing a bed.

1

In these teeming tenements the filth and stench of unemptied privies flowing into the courtyards and the foul air from open sewers were sickening. Disease was rife, but even before it came, such conditions produced physical deterioration and sickliness. The rivers, which were the arteries of the major industrial towns, provided drinking water for their working people. These rivers were also the sewers for 'water closets . . . common drains – the drainings from dung hills, . . . slaughter houses, chemical soap, gas, dung, dye houses . . . spent blue and black dye, pig manure, old urine wash, with all sorts of decomposed animal and vegetable substances'.[2]

Slum housing in Victorian England (engraving by Gustave Doré)

Not just disease, but death was ever present – and came early. In an era of child labour, the average age at death for a labourer in Bolton was 18, in Manchester 17 and in Liverpool 15. Tradesmen fared little better. In Leeds their average age at death was 27, in Bolton 23 and in Manchester 20. In 1830, 1848 and 1866 cholera swept through the country. Burial grounds were overcrowded. Bodies would be crammed on top of one another, often with bones protruding through the soil.

The immigrant labourers from the rural areas knew little of this before they arrived. They were themselves fleeing from the poverty and hunger of their own villages and regions. What they found was employment at workshops in which they would be crowded into tiny suffocating spaces to work for 12, 14 or even 16 hours a day in temperatures 20 or 30 degrees higher than that of the air outside. In the nailers' workshops, seven or eight individuals might work in a space 15 feet long and 12 feet wide, while in a large London tailoring shop, 80 men worked knee to knee in a room 16 or 18 yards long and 7 or 8 yards wide. One report commented:

> The effluvia of these little work dens, from the filthiness on the ground, from the half ragged, half washed persons at work, and from the hot smoke, ashes, water and clouds of dust... are really dreadful.[3]

With this new industrialisation went dramatic increases in production. Coal output and textile manufacture had doubled by the 1830s since the turn of the century, while the output of pig iron had trebled. Many of the old craft industries were wiped out by competition from the new, large-scale manufacturers. The result was misery for those whose trades were destroyed. In 1797 the wages of a Bolton handloom weaver, for example, had stood at 30 shillings and sixpence a week. By 1830 they had fallen to 5 shillings and sixpence. But workers in the newly emerging industries were no happier.

Discipline inside the workshops and factories was oppressive. The artisans of pre-industrial Britain had enjoyed a degree of control over when and how they worked. In good times a weaver or furniture maker might finish the week early if enough trade had been done, and spend the rest of the week in and about the alehouses of the area. Typically, Monday was a day of rest or even revelry. 'St Monday', as it was known, was a well-established tradition. The nailers of the Black Country would throw their hammers in the air, declaring that they would work on Monday if the hammers did not fall. It was such traditions that the factory owners now became determined to stamp out.

In most factories a bewildering array of rules and fines existed, the aim of which was to remove any sense of control for the worker over even the smallest details of production. If an operative sat down for a rest, they might be fined a shilling. If they spoke to another worker or were heard whistling, they could be fined sixpence. Indeed, in one spinning mill in Manchester in 1823, any spinner found 'dirty at his work' could be fined 1 shilling, as could any spinner found washing himself!

If conditions were appalling for adult factory workers, they were all the more so for the children widely employed in the new industries. Legislation regulating the employment of children in the textile industry was included in successive Factory Acts in the first half of the nineteenth century. But less than rigorous enforcement allowed the often ruthless exploitation of children to continue in the mills. Children were particularly valued by the employers for their nimble fingers, which could work the fast-moving, intricate power looms. Orphans as young as six or seven were procured from the workhouses by the factories and industrial workshops. They were regularly subjected to arbitrary discipline and beatings by the overseers. Punishments for lateness or misbehaviour included being hit with an iron rod known as the 'billy-roller', being hung by the hands over the machinery and even having hand vices screwed into their ears.

In the mines, children would be strapped to coal trolleys to crawl on all fours through dangerously narrow tunnels which were prone to cave-ins. Here is a comment from the report of the Children's Employment Commission of 1842:

> *Chained, belted, harnessed like dogs in a go-cart, black, saturated with wet, and more than half-naked – crawling upon their hands and feet, and dragging their heavy loads behind them – they present an appearance indescribably disgusting and unnatural.*[4]

The cry for reform

It is not the case, however, that the workers of the opening years of the nineteenth century accepted their suffering passively. In fact, quite the opposite. These were years of class struggle and the dawning of a broad working-class consciousness that was to form the basis of the first socialist ideas and organisations in Britain.

Time and again the cry went up for political reform. Reform, it was felt, and especially the popular vote, would provide the necessary mechanism by which social wrongs could be redressed. It was not then simply a question of abstract rights and high principle. It was more a question of eliminating the desperate poverty of much of the early industrial working class. As the radical publisher, William Cobbett, put it:

> *reform must be something more than a bill, something more than a bit of paper, it must, to be productive of harmony, cause something to be done to better the state of the people; and, in order to do this, it must produce it quickly too, not only a change*

*in the management in the affairs of the country, but a very great
change . . .*[5]

This desire for reform was to culminate in the Chartist movement in
the late 1830s. But the demand for the popular vote was
longstanding. From as far back as the English Civil War of the
seventeenth century, there had been the demand for annual
parliaments and universal suffrage. But it was with the French
Revolution of 1789 that the inspiration of political reform among
the working class, which was to lead to Chartism, really began.

The revolution in France made a deep impression on urban life in
Britain. The ideals of human rights and equality exploded into the
political life of Europe and registered powerfully in the British
working class. Jacobin clubs sprang up among the artisan
communities, and 'corresponding societies' emerged in the years
immediately following the revolution. The London Corresponding
Society, the most influential of these societies, was established in
1793. Once again the demand for universal suffrage was to the fore.
Prospective members had to agree 'that the welfare of these
kingdoms require that every adult person, in possession of his
reason, and not incapacitated by crimes, should have a vote for a
Member of Parliament'.[6]

Such societies provided a network for the dissemination of
radical and Jacobin ideas among artisans and sections of the lower
middle classes. John Thelwall, who was the most able theorist of the
London Corresponding Society, as well as an outstanding orator and
the toughest of its leaders in the face of government repression,
came close to socialism in his rhetoric.

Mass meetings, demonstrations and food riots were frequent at
the turn of century. In 1795 the king was mobbed by a hostile crowd
in London – an episode that was to be repeated some years later.
The government became obsessed with the possibility of
revolutionary conspiracy. Already there had been mutinies in the
navy at the Nore and at Spithead. The French navy seemed poised to
land on the coast of Ireland. Combinations of workers began to
assume a menacing aspect in the minds of the authorities. In 1799
and 1800 Combination Acts were passed which criminalised any
attempt by workers to organise themselves. The swearing of oaths
was also seen as smacking of revolutionary activity and was
therefore declared illegal.

Uprisings, plots and conspiracies continued right through to
1820. From 1811 to 1813 the Luddite movement shook the
manufacturing districts. Men and women ruined or deskilled by the
factory system took to breaking up the new machinery. The

movement started with the smashing of stocking frames by the stockingers of Nottingham. It spread as a highly organised form of revolt through other districts. Serious confrontations between armed Luddites and owners and troops defending premises occurred in Leicestershire, Derbyshire, Lancashire and Yorkshire. Here again, the political ideas of the Luddites were an admixture of vague notions of insurrection, legislative regulation of their trades and parliamentary reform.

In 1816, in East Anglia, major disturbances and food riots broke out among labourers demanding a minimum wage of 2 shillings a day and price controls. In December of the same year, following a gathering addressed by the popular radical orator and parliamentary reformer Henry Hunt, demonstrators marched from a huge gathering at Spa Fields to the Tower of London, where large-scale rioting occurred.

The following year a mood of insurrection swept through the working-class areas of the north. Working men from Pentridge marched on Nottingham under the stern leadership of one Jeremiah Brandreth. Their aim was to abolish the national debt and establish a provisional government. They were stopped before the city by a force of Hussars.

Similar attempts at uprisings occurred elsewhere, for example at Huddersfield. Expectations of insurrection abounded both in ruling-class circles and among the working class when unemployed textile workers from Lancashire – dubbed the 'Blanketeers' since they each carried a blanket – began their march to London in March 1817. In fact their aim was merely to present a petition to the Prince Regent for reform and the relief of distress. Most were arrested before getting anywhere near the capital.

We get a flavour of what was going on in the following description of the atmosphere of 1815–16:

> In London and Westminster riots ensued, and were continued for several days whilst the [Corn] Bill was discussed; at Bridgeport there were riots on account of the high price of bread; at Bideford, there were similar disturbances to prevent the exploitation of grain; at Bury, by the unemployed, to destroy machinery; at Ely, not suppressed without bloodshed; at Newcastle-on-Tyne, by colliers and others; at Glasgow, where blood was shed; at Preston, by unemployed workers; at Nottingham by Luddites, who destroyed thirty frames; at Merthyr Tydfil, on a reduction of wages; at Birmingham, by the unemployed; and at Dundee where, owing to the high price of meal, upwards of one hundred shops were plundered.[7]

Little wonder it was made a capital offence to 'preach reform to a soldier or to smash a frame'.

The new bourgeoisie of industrial capitalism were alarmed at the ferocity of much working-class revolt they observed. They saw themselves as creators of a dramatically new world of industrial expansion, trade, profit and wealth. And at the heart of this new world was a working class that was growing both in numbers and in consciousness. It was a working class which they feared and which they did not understand. Their loathing was to be vented in the great massacre which occurred at St Peter's Fields, Manchester.

The opening months of 1819 had been marked by enormous mass working-class meetings. These gatherings were remarkable, not for their rowdiness, but for their restraint and discipline. Such a gathering occurred on 16 August at St Peter's Fields. Between 50,000 and 60,000 attended. Different sections of the assembled, all highly organised in their procession, carried banners which bore slogans such as 'Suffrage Universal', 'Parliaments Annual' and 'Liberty and Fraternity'.

The orderly, indeed regimented, appearance of the demonstration was deliberate. The aim of the day was to present the working-class movement in a constitutional light. The very respectability of the procession and others like it was, it was hoped, going to persuade the authorities to introduce political reform. Yet it was precisely this level of organisation that most alarmed the authorities and which provoked the savagery of their response.

On the day itself Henry Hunt had been speaking and the yeomanry had been sent into the crowd to arrest him. A section of the yeomanry was left behind in the crowd and a company of the 15th Hussars, veterans of Waterloo, were sent in to extricate them. Under orders to disperse the crowd the Hussars and the freed yeomanry laid to with their cutlasses, clearing the field within minutes. When they had finished, 11 were dead and 400 lay wounded. 'Peterloo', as it became known, was to live on in the minds of workers for a generation, as a symbol of the violence of which the ruling class was capable. But more than this, workers were drawing the lessons. Despite their attempt to give a respectable face to their movement, despite the peaceful nature of the demonstrations, still they had been hacked down.

The mood for reform developed among the working class throughout the 1820s. When a mass movement once again developed in the early 1830s, with monster gatherings and processions, most eyes were still fixed on Parliament and the reforming MPs and orators. But the reform movement was also accompanied by widespread agitation as expectations of change were raised. Demonstrations of workers occurred all over the country, the largest being of over 100,000 in London and Birmingham. Political unions too, campaigning for reform, sprang up everywhere. Riots were also occurring as the mood for reform took on a revolutionary zeal.

After the rejection of the Reform Bill of 1831, lives were lost when a mob attacked the city prison in Derby and released the prisoners. At Nottingham the castle was burned down. Anti-reformers from the House of Lords could not walk the streets without having to face angry commoners. In October, Sir Charles Wetherall, a prominent opponent of reform in the Commons, made a state entry into Bristol and was greeted by a hostile crowd numbering 10,000. After several police charges, skirmishes broke out and continued for four hours before the Riot Act was read by the mayor. When troops arrived, the crowd was on the offensive and a major confrontation occurred in which the New Jail was attacked, the governor's house destroyed, prisoners set free and the prison itself burned down. Next the Bishop's palace and several other buildings were burnt to ashes. By the fourth morning the military were able to clear the streets. About a hundred had been killed or wounded.

The desire for political reform had reached a frenzied pitch in some areas. When the Duke of Wellington's Tory government fell at the end of 1830, to be replaced by the liberal Whigs, expectations of imminent change rose. They rose further still when the Reform Bill was re-introduced in March of the following year. It was not that the eventual passing of the bill in 1832 gave workers anything at all, since the suffrage it allowed extended only to tenants who paid more than £10 per annum, enfranchising only 50 per cent more men than in 1830. It was simply that its passing was seen as the beginning of a process of extending the franchise into the working class. However, this image of the Whig government heralding a new enlightenment in British society and being a friend of the working classes was very short lived.

The Whigs

In 1833 the Whigs delivered the first shock to those who had looked to them for change, by introducing the Irish Coercion Act. Agitation against British domination had reached a high point in Ireland and the Whigs now introduced a ferociously repressive regime. The Lord Lieutenant was given extraordinary powers to suppress the most ordinary rights of political expression. The point was not lost in radical circles that if such measures could be used in Ireland, they could equally be used anywhere in Britain. Huge open-air rallies were held against the Act in industrial districts, addressed by such working-class orators as John Doherty, the cotton spinners' leader.

The increased repression in Ireland, however, was only the first step in a rapidly growing disillusionment with the new government. The Whigs now delivered a blow to the campaign for a shorter working day. Rejecting any government intervention to reduce the hours worked by adults, the Whigs conceded the principle of reducing the hours worked by children to 8 hours. But a cruel sleight of hand lay behind this 'reform'. In many areas of industry the effect was to increase the working day of those workers whom the children were employed to help. While two children might work 8 hours each over a 16-hour day, the same labourer or craftsman would now have to work the whole 16 hours when the children were available. In fact, not even the children benefited. The reduction in pay that followed a reduction in hours meant that they now worked the same number of hours or more, but for more than one employer.

The employers' offensive under the Whigs was fierce. Labourers were forced to sign the 'document', pledging not to join a trade union. In 1834 six Dorchester labourers were transported for nothing more than forming a trade union branch. These men were to become known as the Tolpuddle Martyrs. Another celebrated case occurred in 1838 when the leaders of the cotton spinners' strike in Glasgow were also transported. The ferocity of the repression effectively smashed general unionism in the 1830s. At the same time, however, it also created heroes and martyrs of the movement. The Tolpuddle Martyrs came back in 1838 to a euphoric reception after a vigorous campaign on their behalf. The Whigs had demonstrated a violence and hostility towards the working class which had banished any illusions that workers had of them. But there was one Act of the Whigs which came to symbolise their contempt for the lower orders and which was to galvanise working-class anger more than any other. This was the Poor Law Amendment Act of 1834.

Poverty levels were already appalling in British society, and were rising steeply in the 1830s. One quarter of Carlisle's population was on the brink of starvation. Of a total population of 9,000 in Accrington, only 100 had full-time jobs. Whole families were living on nothing but boiled nettles. Poor relief was consuming a hefty £7 million of the national purse in 1832. The Whigs now set out to slash this figure.

*Victorian
workhouses:
'a terror to
the poor'*

The most fashionable ideas of the time on the question of the poor were those of Thomas Malthus. He argued that it was not possible for society to feed the hungry and that it was folly to give relief, since this only worsened the problem. The new Poor Law replaced localised relief and introduced a new, centralised system. Those who could not support themselves had to enter newly established workhouses. The object of these workhouses was, in the words of one assistant commissioner, 'to establish therein a discipline so severe and repulsive as to make them a terror to the poor and prevent them from entering'. Families were torn apart. Husbands were separated from their wives and children from their parents. Healthy and diseased were confined together in tiny areas. In some, eight to ten people would occupy a single sleeping space. Three or four mothers with their newborn babies shared a single bed. The 'Andover scandal' of 1845–6 later came to symbolise what the workhouses represented. Riots occurred when inmates began to fight over scraps of meat on bones they had been given to grind.

The effect of the Poor Law of 1834 was to drive further masses of workers into absolute destitution. The bastardy clause removed all support for the mother unless she could prove the identity of the father in court. The despair of the most poverty-stricken of the time is well illustrated by the growth of children's burial clubs. Sunday school pupils contributed one penny a week towards their own or a fellow pupil's funeral. This period also saw the dissemination of a pamphlet, perhaps satirical, by 'Marcus', which advocated infanticide.

The new Poor Law achieved its goal. By 1841 the cost of poor relief had been drastically reduced. It had achieved something else, however. A polarisation had occurred in society which was perhaps unprecedented. The working class saw with a new clarity the way in which their rulers viewed them. Revolts had already occurred in the industrial regions of Cheshire, Yorkshire, Lancashire and Carlisle. In Kent a semi-religious movement occurred against the Poor Law. The leader was an ex-brewer named Thom of Canterbury, who, having arrived in that town in 1832 wearing Eastern dress, proclaimed himself to be: Sir William Courtenay; King of the Gypsies; Knight of Malta; King of Jerusalem; and the Messiah. Even under the leadership of a madman, workers would fight to the death, as many on this occasion did, to overthrow the Poor Law. The Revd J. R. Stephens – the dissenting ex-Wesleyan preacher and one of the movement's most inflammatory speakers at that time – addressed crowds of up to 100,000 with a fiery rhetoric. Speaking at Newcastle he proclaimed that, in response to the Poor Law and the workhouse, equally it should be law:

> for every man to have his firelock, his cutlass, his sword, his pair of pistols or his pike, and for every woman to have her pair of scissors, and for ever[y] child to have its paper of pins and its box of needles, and let the men with torch in one hand and a dagger in the other put to death any and all who attempt to sever man and wife.[8]

From reform to the Charter

By the late 1830s, the hopes inspired by the Reform Bill of 1832 seemed a very distant memory. In 1832 workers had hoped for an improvement in their living standards and for the vote. The Whig government, however, had displayed a cruel disregard for the poor and no inclination whatever to extend the franchise. As the petition from Thomas Attwood, MP for Birmingham, put it: 'They have been bitterly and basely deceived. The fruit which had looked so fair to the eye has turned to dust and ashes when gathered.'[9]

What many workers now realised was that there was within the middle and upper classes a deep hostility towards the extension of the vote beyond very narrow limits. This class hostility even permeated the thinking of the reformers. The liberalism of the nineteenth-century reform movement was rooted ultimately in a desire to trade freely, unhindered by religious orthodoxy or state interference. It had very little to do with democracy. Even the more radical democrats, such as John Stuart Mill, saw education as a necessary precondition of extending the vote. In his opinion, widening the franchise:

> places the principle of power in the hands of classes more and more below the highest level of instruction in the ... community ... it is hurtful that the constitution of the country should declare ignorance to be entitled to as much political power as knowledge.[10]

This portrayal of the working class as an ignorant, uneducated mob was actually quite wrong. The struggles of the opening years of the nineteenth century, which had produced such sharp class polarisation in British society, had also provided the backdrop for something of an enlightenment in the working-class districts. Great importance began to be attached to the ability to read, and a thirst for self-improvement pervaded the working-class radicalism of the time. Workers who had laboured 10, 11 or even 12-hour days would then work into the night, by the light of a candle, reading Shakespeare or books on the sciences of the day or on the latest continental philosophy. Many would meet in rooms to read and discuss the most current radical pamphlets. The Barnsley weavers, who paid a penny a month to buy radical journals, were typical. Coffee houses such as John Doherty's 'Coffee and Newsroom' in Manchester became popular as centres where political pamphlets could be purchased and read in public.

Radical periodicals such as the *Weekly Political Register* and the *Black Dwarf* enjoyed circulations of tens of thousands in working-class districts. Such publications gave voice to a growing class consciousness on the part of workers and artisans. This was not lost on the authorities of the day who, in an attempt to silence the movement, imposed severe taxes on working-class publications, effectively putting them beyond the reach of workers. All newspapers were henceforth made to carry a government stamp showing that the tax had been paid. Some papers, such as the *Black Dwarf,* moderated their tone in the hope of avoiding government repression, and lost circulation in the process. There were others, however, such as the publisher Richard Carlile, who declared open defiance of the tax. Unstamped newspapers and journals appeared all over the country. Publishers and vendors were tried and incarcerated in the most appalling conditions, leaving dependants with no means of support. Far from quelling the movement, however, this repression seemed to fuel it. More publications and periodicals appeared – *The Operative*, the *Northern Liberator*, *Tribune of the People*, the *London Democrat*, *The Extinguisher*, the *Plain Speaker*, *Friend of the People*, *Reynolds Political Instructor*, and the *Unfettered Thinker and Plain Speaker for Truth, Freedom and Progress*, among many others.

The 'battle of the unstamped', as it became known, was important in preparing the ground for the Chartist movement which followed soon after. Networks of those trading and taking the periodicals of the day developed in every city and small town; a nucleus of radical workers and artisans became established. Often these were centred around a coffee house or inn, where the most important, topical or interesting articles would be read aloud for the benefit of those who were illiterate. The movement also began to create a leadership within working-class communities. On a national level, figures began to emerge who would be crucial in the tumultuous years ahead. In 1836 a new national body was formed. The Association of Working Men to Procure a Cheap and Honest Press emerged as the first national voice of the radical press. A few months later this was to grow into the London Working Men's Association (LWMA).

The LWMA was initially a fairly theoretical organisation. It addressed issues of social and political concern and sought to achieve change through the gradual edification of workers by the written word. Indeed, a certain elitism pervaded its view of the masses it had set itself to improving. The 'drunken and immoral' were explicitly excluded, and membership was to be restricted to the 'honest, sober, moral and thinking portion of our brethren'. In the climate of the late 1830s, however, it could not remain such a body for long. The struggles of the 1830s to defend trade unions, to oppose the factory system and Poor Law, and for the right to a free working-class press were crystallising rapidly in the minds of workers towards one idea. What had been fought against were aspects of the system. What had to be changed was the political system itself. The Whigs had failed to deliver reform, and now workers had to take the issue into their own hands. Propelled forward by this new political momentum, the LWMA called together an assemblage at the Crown and Anchor pub in the Strand on 28 February 1837. The purpose was to adopt a list of demands around which to gather a monster petition for democratic reform – a charter – which would be presented to Parliament. It is from this meeting that the story of Chartism proper begins. James Bronterre O'Brien, veteran of the unstamped movement, and later to become one of the most important Chartist leaders, has left us the following account:

> *Four thousand democrats at least were present at the meeting. The immense meeting hall of the Crown and Anchor was full to over flowing, several hundred stood outside on the corridor and stairs, or went away for want of accommodation . . . The arrangements of the committee were in every respect complete, and of the true democratic stamp. A working man was appointed to preside. The resolutions and petitions were severally proposed and seconded by working men. The principal speakers who supported them were working men. The petition itself . . . was drawn up by working men. In short, the whole proceedings were originated, conducted, and concluded by working men and that in a style which would have done credit to any assembly in the world.*[11]

The Charter adopted was constituted of five demands:

1. *Equal representation.* The UK was to be divided into 200 electoral districts of roughly equal population, each sending a representative to Parliament.
2. *Universal suffrage.* Every person over 21 years of age would be entitled to vote. (This was later to be changed to every man of 21 years or over.)
3. *Annual parliaments.* A general election was to be held every year on 24 June.
4. *No property qualifications.* Standing in an election was not to be dependent on possessions or property.
5. *Vote by ballot.* Voting was to be in secret to ensure that allegiances could not be bought and sold, and to eliminate patronage and intimidation by employers.

Today such demands seem unremarkable. In 1837, however, they sent shock waves through the ruling class. The Charter was to become a lightning conductor which channelled the energy and anger of a generation of struggle.

Working Men of Every Clime

Working men of every clime,
Gather still, but bide your time,
Bide your time, and wait a wee,
Yours will be the victory.

Britain's sons, whose constant toil,
Plies the loom and tills the soil,
Lift the voice for liberty,
Yours will be the victory.

Toil-worn sons of Spain advance,
Give the hand to those of France,
Join you both with Italy,
Yours will be the victory.

Serfs of Poland, gather near,
Raise, with Austria's sons, the cheer,
Echo'd far through Germany,
Yours will be the victory.

Danish workmen, hear the cry,
Scandinavia's quick reply,
Workmen, 'panting to be free',
Yours will be the victory ...

Dutchmen, linger not behind,
Working men should be combined,
Russian slaves themselves will see,
Yours will be the victory.

Europe's workmen; one and all,
Rouse ye at your brethren's call,
Shouting loud from sea to sea,
Yours will be the victory.

Kings and nobles may conspire,
God will pour on them his ire;
Workmen shout, for ye are free,
Yours is now the victory.

Northern Star, 28 November 1840

Chapter 2   The Newport rising: 1839

'Physical force' versus 'moral force'

The national launch of the Charter occurred on 4 February 1839 at the British Coffee House in Cockburn Street, London, on the occasion of the first Chartist Convention. In the language of the nineteenth century, the notion of the 'convention' meant something more than a meeting of like-minded people. From the middle of the eighteenth century, a 'convention' had come to mean an alternative Parliament in a political society that disenfranchised the vast majority. It was a representative assembly invested with political authority by its members.

If the intention was to be a representative assembly, however, the reality was somewhat different. The makeup of the gathering at the British Coffee House – it was to move to Bolt Court, off Fleet Street, two days later – reflected little of the storm of working-class revolt that was brewing within British society. Fifty-four delegates were present. The majority were solidly middle class – business men, preachers, medical men, a lawyer, booksellers and so on. Perhaps 24 of those present could have been described as 'working men' according to the old radical tailor and chronicler of the working-class movement, Francis Place. This conflicting social mix was to influence subsequent proceedings.

The conservatism of the early leadership had already been demonstrated by a change that had been made to the original draft of the Charter. Along with the addition of a sixth point – the payment of Members of Parliament in order that working-class members could afford to take their seats in the House – the demand for universal suffrage was no longer present. The first point of the Charter now demanded 'A vote for every man twenty-one years of age, of sound mind, and not undergoing punishment for crime'. Leading moderates such as William Lovett had held that to call for the vote for women was to go too far too fast. Many felt that doing so could alienate middle-class support.

The distance between the leadership and the mass movement that was swelling behind the Charter was now reflected at the Convention. After some preliminary matters had been addressed and reports made – it was announced, for example, that over half a million signatures had already been collected for the Charter – the discussion moved on to what precisely the purpose of the Convention was to be. Now the tensions broke through.

The London leaders were keen for the Convention to restrict itself merely to overseeing the collection of signatures for the petition and presenting it to Parliament. They were explicitly opposed to the Convention straying outside this minimal role to involve itself in questions of economic injustice or advocacy of any brand of socialism. Other delegates railed against the Convention being limited in this way. Surely, they insisted, the Convention had to address itself urgently to the question of what was to be done in the very likely event of the Charter's rejection by Parliament? How was the Convention to lead a movement that was heading towards a confrontation with the Whigs and what 'ulterior measures' might be taken to force their hand? The delegates from the Midlands, alarmed at this kind of talk, now withdrew from the Convention altogether.

Underlying these divisions were fundamental differences of outlook as to how the battle was to be fought. The moderates believed that the Whigs could be persuaded to introduce reform. The way forward, they argued, was through the patient stating and restating of the case. The petition alone and, for some, the sympathy of the middle class would be enough to demonstrate the moral superiority of their argument.

Against these 'moral force' Chartists stood those who had no such illusions about either the sympathy of the middle class for their cause or the amenability of the government to change. Expecting the Convention itself to be broken up by the authorities at any time, the 'physical force' Chartists now looked to their strengths. What force might they themselves use against a government that had demonstrated many times its willingness to use repression when threatened? Most favoured was an idea taken from the widely influential pamphlet by William Benbow entitled *Grand National Holiday*. Benbow had advocated a general withdrawal of labour, or 'Sacred Month', the aim of which was to demonstrate that labour is the source of all wealth. A general strike was to be the response of the Convention to government provocation.

The manifesto issued by the Convention also addressed the following questions to the localities: would they, on request by the Convention, withdraw all monies from banks? would they provide candidates for a general election? would they rally round any Chartist victimised by the authorities? had they prepared to defend their rights with arms?

The debate was far from being academic. As the Convention moved to Birmingham, events were gathering pace. Huge mobilisations were occurring around the country. In May 1838 a two-mile procession around 200,000-strong, including 70 trade unions, 43 bands and 300 banners, had ended at Glasgow Green in the Scottish city, and had declared for the Charter, as had others at the time. Gatherings and processions were happening all over the country to do the same. The largest were at Newcastle Town Moor, Peep Green in West Riding and Kersal Moor outside Manchester.

The mood of these events cannot be simply explained in terms of a revolt against material deprivation or just a desire to achieve the vote. Beneath the surface boiled a ferment of emotions and aspirations within the working class for something better than they had. Their demands were not only political but also social. In a fictitious dialogue published by the Finsbury Tract Society in 1839, a 'Mr Radical' proclaimed as demands of the Charter:

> *The abolition of the enormous abuses of the civil and criminal law, which amount in most cases to an utter denial of justice to the poor; a liberal and general system of national education, without reference to sect or creed, which would tend at once to diminish crime, by striking at its root. The cost of the civil and criminal justice in this country is above two millions, while only £30,000 is devoted to national education.*[1]

The tensions in British society continued to mount. Rioting had occurred at Llanidloes and took place again in Birmingham after police had attacked the crowds who had regularly been waiting in the Bull Ring for news of the Convention. The Home Office was inundated by reports of arming and drilling going on outside the major industrial areas. A Bolton magistrate reported that:

> *a large number of pikes was in the course of being manufactured in the town . . . there is no attempt to conceal the making of them for two of the workshops are at the front of the street and the men are seen at work by all passers by . . . in the last few days the demand for them has increased greatly and generally . . . There have been meetings every night for the last week and every means used to influence the lower class.*[2]

From the Liverpool Summer Assizes the brief for the prosecution reported a witness's observations of Chartist activities at Ashton-under-Lyne:

they formed themselves into squads ... there were three squads and about thirty or forty in a squad ... the men went through what [the] witness who has been a soldier calls facings ... they formed sections and marched in line across the field and wheeled to the right and marched forward and wheeled again both right and left.[3]

The air was thick with rumours and expectation of insurrection. The atmosphere is well captured by General Napier, commander of the Northern troops who, in counselling a policy of caution, commented that:

There is among the manufacturing poor a stern look of discontent, of hatred to all who are rich, a total absence of merry faces: a sallow tinge and dirty skins tell of suffering and brooding over change ... [4]

Britain's rulers had observed with horror the revolution in France in 1830 and Napier was genuinely worried at the prospect of revolution in Britain. The troops, he warned, had to be kept in large groups, concentrated strategically in the manufacturing districts rather than being scattered in small formations. 'The Chartists are numerous,' he wrote, 'and should one detachment be destroyed the soldiers would lose confidence; they would be shaken, while the rebels would be exalted beyond measure...'[5]

Such then was the mood of 1839. Now what was critical was the resolve of the leaders. The first petition, carrying 1,280,000 signatures, had been presented to Parliament by the radical MPs Thomas Attwood and John Fielden on 17 June. Predictably, it had been overwhelmingly rejected by the House of Commons. At the same time the Convention itself had been declared illegal and Chartist leaders were being arrested. The delegates responded by calling the 'Sacred Month' on 17 July.

Now, however, fresh acrimony broke out. The Convention, which was meeting again in London, far from the centres of revolt, was an untested and divided leadership of a dramatically growing and clearly explosive movement. The majority of delegates, including many of those who had declared for 'physical force' Chartism, were frankly unprepared for an all-or-nothing confrontation with the Whigs. Suddenly doubting their ability to sustain a general strike for as long as a month, they stepped back from the brink.

Armed revolt

The call now went out for a National Holiday of three days. The 'long weekend' of 10–13 August saw widespread strike action around the country. This was certainly enough to alarm the authorities about the threat they were facing, but it was not enough to force them to retreat. Mass arrests of leaders and local activists now occurred. The Convention, reeling under the onslaught, began to crumble and was finally suspended on 6 August.

'Respectable' society was jubilant. It appeared that Chartism and the spectre of revolution it raised had been laid to rest. Their celebrations, however, were short-lived. What had ended was not Chartism itself but merely its opening scene. The one that was to follow was to develop into one of the most serious threats to the establishment in British history. But now the centre of attention swung towards the valleys of South Wales.

Chartism and other forms of radical politics and militancy had already gained strong influence in the industrial regions of Wales. In the 1820s and 1830s, the 'Scotch Cattle' had meted out punishment to those who opposed workers' combinations. The 'Cattle', most of them colliers, were organised into 'herds' in almost every working-class district. Led by a 'bull', they would approach the home of a particularly hostile employer, or unsympathetic shopkeeper, or even a collier who refused to support the union, disguised in animal skins and announcing their presence and their intention to deal out rough justice with animal sounds.

In the 1830s, conditions for industrial workers in Wales were as miserable as anywhere else in Britain. In massively overcrowded communities, housing and sanitation were in a deplorable state. Food prices were high, wages were low and cholera stalked the valleys. In the mines, work would begin at 3 or 4 a.m. and finish at 8 or 9 p.m. Miners were frequently paid not with money but with tokens to be exchanged for inferior goods at high prices in company shops. It is small wonder that the mood of grim resentment which pervaded the working-class communities of Wales was to break through into active revolt, as it had in the past.

At Merthyr Tydfil in 1831, during the agitation around the first Reform Bill, thousands of industrial workers had staged an insurrection under a red flag. They drove out a division of Argyll and Sutherland Highlanders and held the area for four days. The rising was finally crushed by 800 troops with the loss of 24 workers' lives.

Now, in 1839, after a winter of bad harvests and a state of semi-starvation in the rural areas, revolt was in the air once again. In May the first 'Rebecca Riots' had occurred. Tollgates, newly introduced on roads in the western counties, became a focus for the anger felt in the region. They were destroyed by mobs of several hundred, disguised, with blackened faces and wearing women's clothing. The authorities despaired as special constables sworn in to protect the gates fled in terror to the fields, and the gates were finally removed. The Rebeccas were not seen again until 1842 when their activities produced a state of near civil war with the authorities.

The industrial areas of South Wales were strongholds of Chartism. Support had grown among the weavers of Montgomeryshire, who were being pushed out of their trade by the competition of English produce, and among the miners of Gwent and Glamorgan. One of the first centres of Chartism had been Merthyr Tydfil. The editor of the *Merthyr Telegraph* had claimed that their strength was negligible. The Merthyr Chartists took up the challenge by attending and filling out the parish church in full uniform of Welsh fabrics. The peculiarly Welsh character of Chartism in the valleys was also symbolised in the figure of the Pontypridd leader, Dr William Price. Price was a Welsh nationalist and devotee of Druidism, who dressed only in Welsh fabrics, wore a mediaeval sword and attended Chartist processions in a carriage pulled by four goats.

In the atmosphere following the rejection of the first petition, expectations and rumours of insurrection were rife. As the arrests continued, plans were afoot for risings in most of the industrial areas around the country. Henry Vincent, the enormously popular 'physical force' orator, had toured South Wales advocating defiance of government repression, finishing one of his speeches with the words, 'Perish the privileged orders! Death to the aristocracy.' His arrest in London was not long in coming and he was returned to Wales for trial.

The arrest of Vincent had an electrifying effect. Preparations for a rising began in earnest. Illegal forges were operating, manufacturing weapons in the remote caves of the Welsh hills. Chartist workers were drilling and rehearsing military tactics. Detailed planning took place in the public houses of West Monmouthshire. Under the leadership of Zephaniah Williams, William Jones and, principally, John Frost, they were to march in three separate divisions through the working-class towns of Pontypool and Risca, converge on Newport and release Vincent and the other arrested Chartists.

Probably 20,000 took part in the march through the pouring rain on the night of 3 November 1839. Some came from nearly 20 miles away to take part. They were organised into brigades, companies and units – the largest unit being 1,485 strong including officers. The chain of command went from John Frost, who was commander-in-chief, down to the corporals and deacons in each unit. The password for the night was 'Beanswell'. A stranger greeted with the word 'Beans' had to reply with 'Well' or face 'arrest'. One who was arrested, and was not at all sympathetic to either the Chartists or the rising, has left us with the following account of the section under John Frost's immediate command, which:

> consisted of several thousands of men, nearly all armed, some with pikes, fixed on well made handles or shafts, some more roughly made; crude spears formed of rod iron sharpened at one end, and turned into a loop at the other as a handle; guns, muskets, pistols, coal mandrills [sharp double-pointed pick axes used in cutting coal], clubs, scythes, crowbars; and, in fact, any and everything that they could lay their hands on. The whole represented one of the most heterogeneous collections of instruments and munitions of war that ever were brought into the field to compete with disciplined and well-armed forces.[6]

While our witness has a point regarding the military preparedness of the Chartist workers, it cannot be overstated that what was occurring was a completely serious, large-scale attempt at a planned insurrection. The intention, or more precisely the hope, was that it would coincide with or spark similar risings elsewhere in the country.

As the tension mounted, the well-to-do of the area were seized by panic. One local minister hid himself overnight in an ironworks feeder, up to his chin in murky water. On the morning of 4 November, 5,000 Chartists entered Newport. A combination of exhaustion, ambiguous instructions and indiscipline meant that the majority of the marchers did not get as far as the town itself. Certainly the public houses on the route of the march had not contributed to good order. However, nothing now could prevent the conflict. Still under Frost's command, the marchers proceeded to the Westgate Hotel where a division of soldiers had been stationed to protect the town.

Accounts of what precisely followed are somewhat confused. What is clear, however, is that, after an exchange of words between the insurgents and those inside the hotel, fighting broke out. There was an explosion of gunfire from both sides, Chartists broke through the main door and fighting occurred inside the building. In the space of perhaps 15 minutes, as many as 24 Chartists were killed or

The Newport rising, 1839

mortally wounded. The Chartists fell back in disarray and fled. Bodies of the dead and wounded lay in front of the hotel with abandoned weapons scattered around them. The insurrection was over.

The impact of defeat

Over the next few days, rumours circulated of a second attempt, but with the arrest of Frost and the other leaders there was very little serious prospect. A rising in Bradford that had been supposed to coincide with that at Newport had not happened because its leadership had lost their nerve and called it off. As news of Frost's arrest spread, Chartists in Manchester, Bradford, Sheffield, Halifax, Dewsbury and Newcastle began to talk of a Northern rising. Attempts at further risings took place in Sheffield, where police were attacked, and in Bradford in January 1840. With the defeat at Newport, however, the momentum had been lost and neither episode approached the scale or seriousness of that event.

Chartist leaders around the country were now being rounded up by the authorities. Between January 1839 and June 1840 nearly 500 Chartists were arrested. More than 250 received prison sentences and six, including Frost, were sentenced to death. The authorities, worried at the prospect of inciting further revolt, later commuted the sentences to deportation for life.

Since the rising, fact has blended with myth as to its background. At the time, rumours circulated that it had been the work of government spies and *agents provocateurs*. Since then historians anxious to deny a revolutionary tradition in the British working class have trivialised the significance of the events at Newport, referring to them as a riot or even a mere protest.

That the Newport rising, also in effect a general strike, was a genuine attempt to overthrow the authority of the day and establish the Charter, however, is indisputable when we look at the evidence. The secrecy surrounding the preparations was unprecedented. Communications and visits between South Wales and the working-class districts of the North proceeded at a furious pace in the days before the attempt. As many as 600 of the insurgents carried firearms of some description, which they regularly tested on the road and loaded just before they entered the town. Many were fully aware of the possibility that they might die in their bid for freedom. George Shell, a 19-year-old cabinet maker who was shot dead at the Westgate Hotel, wrote to his parents before he set out on the march:

> I shall this night be engaged in a struggle for freedom, and should it please God to spare my life I shall see you soon; but if not, grieve not for me, I shall fall in a noble cause. My tools are at Mr Cecil's, and likewise my clothes.[7]

A scheme had been considered to stage revolts at Brecon, Abergavenny and Cardiff. Zephaniah Williams wrote of a plan to overthrow the government and establish a British republic. There was certainly a general notion that if the attempt were successful, the next step would be the setting up of a Chartist 'Executive Government of England' with Frost as president.

The British working class did not enter the stage of history as passive and marginal players in a predetermined role. They did not go like sheep to the slaughter that was the industrial revolution. Rather they were born in rage. But their fury was not a simple reaction to their oppression. It was channelled into a political idea – the Charter.

The real legacy of the Newport rising, then, is what it tells us of the early working class in Britain. Far from accepting their destiny, workers were grappling with questions of power and class, and by the late 1830s the most advanced part of the industrial working class was consciously revolutionary.

The impact of the defeat at Newport was massive. As the movement reeled under arrests and state repression, the old divisions and tensions which had lain under the surface now began to break out. New forms of Chartism began to emerge as different strands within the movement groped for a new direction. In some areas, Chartist chapels sprang up as a part of the movement associated itself with working-class Methodism. A closely related development was the advocacy of temperance, self-improvement and education.

A new national organisation now emerged. The National Charter Association (NCA) was founded in Manchester on 20 July 1840, under the leadership of Feargus O'Connor. This was to grow into the organisational backbone of the movement. By April 1842 the NCA could claim some 400 localities and 50,000 members, and an influence way beyond these numbers.

A short time after the founding of the NCA, a rival body was set up. The Complete Suffrage Union (CSU) was significant in anticipating the divisions and development of the movement in the later 1840s. The CSU advocated an alliance with the middle classes as the means of achieving political rights, and launched its own petition to this end. Its respectability and courting of middle-class opinion, however, made little impression on Parliament. The CSU petition was overwhelmingly rejected in April 1842. The following month a second Chartist petition with over three million signatures was similarly rejected.

In the months following the 1839 rising, despite its defeat, Chartism was increasing its influence and national spread. Its organisational coherence also improved. The movement was politicising ever wider layers of the working class. This politicisation was now to find a sharp focus in the general strike of August 1842, which once again posed a profound challenge to early industrial capitalism – but now on a massive scale.

The Voice of the People

'Tis the voice of the people I hear it on high;
It peals o'er the mountains – it soars to the sky;
Through wide fields of heather; it wings its swift flight,
Like thunders of heaven arrayed in their might.
It rushes still on, like the torrent's wide roar,
And bears on its surges the wrongs of the poor.
Its shock like the earthquake shall fill with dismay,
The hearts of the tyrants and sweep them away.

Northern Star, 4 December 1841

Chapter 3   The first general strike: 1842

Manchester and the Lancashire workers

No new idea emerges from a vacuum. Rather ideas crystallise against a background of the social flux of the time. So it was with Benbow's advocacy of the general strike in his influential pamphlet on the subject, *Grand National Holiday and Congress of the Productive Classes*. Mass strikes had been seen periodically in the opening years of the nineteenth century. General and near general strikes had occurred on a regional basis among, for example, textile workers in Scotland in 1812 and among Lancashire workers in 1818. Benbow, a self-educated shoemaker, had been an active organiser in such working-class actions. His own home town of Middleton had seen violent confrontations between armed workers and troops. It was from this context that the idea of a genuinely general strike, involving every section of workers across industry, emerged. From the publication of the pamphlet, however, more than a decade was to elapse before Lancashire workers turned the idea into a reality.

By the mid-nineteenth century, Manchester was by far the largest and most important industrial city in the world, and was in effect the second capital of Britain. In his eulogy to the city, Thomas Carlyle was to write:

> *Hast thou heard, with sound ears, the awakening of Manchester on a Monday morning, at half past five by the clock; the rushing off of its thousand mills, like the boom of an Atlantic tide, ten thousand times ten thousand spools and spindles all set humming there – it is perhaps, if thou knew it well, sublime as a Niagara or more so.*[1]

Manchester industry had not only expanded in size since the industrial revolution, but also become more concentrated. The textile industry was more advanced than any other, and by 1841, 93 per cent of the city's 40,000 cotton operatives worked in factories employing more than 100 workers.[2] This concentration of workers had provided the basis of a strong working-class consciousness and

Manchester had in many senses become a leading centre of radical politics. There had been the radical movement of 1816–20 which had ended with the Peterloo massacre. There had also been the agitation in support of the Reform Bill. Now Manchester was to take the lead once again.

The conditions for an explosion of working-class unrest had been developing since the collapse of the boom of 1836. Living standards for workers had fallen dramatically from an already very low level. By June 1837, 50,000 workers in Manchester were unemployed or on short time. Some of the weavers, who petitioned over their plight, had only one penny a day to live on. With the following words Frederick Engels summed up his vivid account of the truly shocking conditions of the Manchester working class:

> *If we briefly formulate the result of our wanderings, we must admit that 350,000 working people of Manchester and its environs live, almost all of them, in wretched, damp, filthy cottages, that the streets which surround them are usually in the most miserable and filthy condition, laid out without the slightest reference to ventilation, with reference solely to the profit secured by the contractor. In a word, we must confess that in the working men's dwellings of Manchester, no cleanliness, no convenience, and consequently no comfortable family life is possible; that in such dwellings only a physically degenerate race, robbed of all humanity, degraded, reduced morally and physically to bestiality, could feel at home.*[3]

Soon, however, the Lancashire workers were to demonstrate both their humanity and their power. By 1842 resentment at the privileged lifestyles of the mill and factory owners was seething. Demands for better wages and conditions met with a contemptuous response. Did the workers not understand the problems faced by industry in a time of depression? Were they completely ignorant of the realities of the trade cycle? Such attitudes were expressed unapologetically in papers such as the *Manchester Times*. But a local song of the time captures well the answer of the poor to such sentiments:

> *How little can the rich man know,*
> *Of what the poor man feels,*
> *When Want, like some dark demon foe,*
> *Nearer and nearer steals!*
> *He never saw his darlings lie,*
> *Shivering, the flags their bed;*

> He never heard that maddening cry
> 'Daddy, a bit of bread!'[4]

The Manchester factory owners, however, did not understand that their operatives could be pushed too far. The drastic attack they now proposed against the working class of the district was to release this anger and trigger the first ever really general strike staged by industrial workers.

In the recession-hit textile industry, the talk among the manufacturers was of wage cuts. Some talked of cuts as high as 27 per cent if they were to compete with their European rivals. Eventually a cut of 12½ per cent was agreed by the factory owners. Textile operatives, hatters, coalminers and engineers had already fought wage cuts, generally without success. The anger among the working-class communities now became sharply focused on the attack on wages and the pace of events quickened once more. Colliers in Staffordshire were already on strike against wage cuts. Now meetings of workers were called to discuss the employers' offensive.

The 'turn-outs'

As the tension mounted, it was to take only one further provocation by the employers to tip the situation into a decisive confrontation. This was not long in coming. The cotton masters of the towns of Stalybridge and Ashton-under-Lyne now announced that wages were to be reduced by 25 per cent. This act of supreme over-confidence was to explode in their faces on a scale they could not have dreamt of.

The textile workers of Stalybridge struck and gathered to discuss what they were to do next. Meetings were called on Mottram Moor over the weekend of 5–7 August. Resolutions were passed demanding 'a fair day's pay for a fair day's work' and pledging not to return to work until the Charter had become the law of the land. Speakers began to talk of 'turning out' workers from the factories and mills of the surrounding districts. On Monday 8 August, 14,000 strikers gathered again on Mottram Moor. But this time they did not return home. Instead, forming themselves into an orderly procession, they began to march. The strikers carried banners and placards along the way. One placard read, 'They that perish by the sword are better than they that perish by hunger.' Thus the 'turn-outs' had begun.

News of what was afoot went ahead of the marchers. As they approached the mills, their singing could be heard and the mill hands inside began to put on their coats and gather their belongings. No argument was required. Factory overseers stood by helpless as their workers walked out to join the turn-outs. At many of the mills, the plugs on the boilers which provided the machines with power were pulled out to ensure that they remained closed down. By two o'clock that afternoon, all the mills of the district had stopped working. Forty thousand assembled at Ashton to hear the aims of the strike reaffirmed, then separated to move off in different directions to other towns.

The following day the strikers approached Manchester in procession. If Manchester fell to the turn-outs, the impact would carry the strike forward beyond the industrial counties where it had begun. This point was not lost on the authorities which, dazed by the suddenness of the outbreak and by the speed of events, were gripped by panic. There were those such as the old military campaigner Sir Charles Shaw, who bayed for the strike to be put down in blood. The Manchester magistrates, however, were alarmed in the extreme at the prospect of a repeat of Peterloo and its possible consequences. They attempted to negotiate with the strikers, but to no avail. These half-starved people, burning with the bitterness of a generation of suffering and insult, were not to be so easily dissuaded from the path on which they had embarked. The turn-outs rolled on into Manchester.

As workers turned out from each factory and mill, they moved on to their neighbours in a kind of chain reaction which raced through the city. Here and there employers and factory managers would put up resistance by attempting to lock their employees in or, in some cases, hurling bricks and concrete from the factory roofs down on to the strikers below. Clashes were now occurring with police, who were utterly overwhelmed. As the strikers proceeded, mass meetings were held in which the Charter was again proclaimed. By the end of the second day of the strike, the whole of Manchester had been closed down. The Chartist Thomas Cooper gives us the reaction of Chartist leaders as they approached Manchester by train:

> So soon as the City of long chimneys came in sight, and every chimney was beheld smokeless, Campbell's [Secretary of the NCA] face changed, and with an oath he said 'Not a single mill at work! Something must come out of this, and something serious too!'[5]

The turn-outs now proceeded out of Manchester on to other industrial towns including Rochdale, Eccles and Halifax. At Stockport the workhouse was attacked, the inmates were released and bread, which was being stored there, was distributed among the strikers. The mass meetings, such as that of around 40,000 at Rochdale, also continued. Troops were now pouring into the region. Serious clashes occurred at Halifax and Blackburn. At Preston at least four people were killed when troops opened fire. A Royal Proclamation offered a £50 reward for the apprehension and conviction of the strike leaders. Yet still the strike spread and by 15 August 250,000 workers were out. Over the following week the strike was to involve over 500,000 workers – perhaps one half of the country's industrial workforce.

What is remarkable about this first phase of the turn-outs is both the immediate politicisation that occurred among the workers involved and their conscious awareness of what they were doing. The predominant view of the turn-outs has been that they were really no more than a spontaneous outburst of anger by workers driven to a frenzy by the attack on wages – nothing at all to do with Chartism. Such a historical view fits cosily with the notion that politics have no place in the trade union battle over the 'purely economic' matters of wages and conditions. In fact, when we look at the discussions that went on among the strikers and the repeated calls for the implementation of the Charter at the mass meetings, it is clear that the Charter featured largely in the strikers' understanding of their actions. The second great Chartist petition, carrying over three million signatures, had been overwhelmingly rejected by Parliament in May. The strike was now seen as a weapon with which to achieve political change. Of the 43 recorded speeches made at meetings in the run-up to the strike, from 26 July to 7 August, only two were by speakers who were not Chartists.[6] The working-class movement in Britain, then, was born a political movement, struggling not only for better pay and conditions, but for social change.

Another dramatic feature of the turn-outs was the involvement of women. Very often it was women strikers, marching in their own contingents, who turned out workers from the mills and factories to join the strike. Often they were the most courageous among the strikers, jeering at police who arrested them and on one celebrated occasion grabbing the bayonets of troops with the cry, 'We want not bayonets, but bread!'

Women workers made up a large percentage of the workforce of early industrial Britain and a tradition of women's activity in the radical movement had already developed even before the rise of Chartism. Women were involved, for example, in the campaign against the Poor Law. In February 1838 the women of Elland had rolled one of the most unpopular commissioners in the snow when he tried to implement the Poor Law in Yorkshire. With the beginning of the Chartist movement, women's Chartist societies and political unions mushroomed around the country. The first Female Charter Association was founded in Birmingham in 1838. Its membership reached 1,300 and it organised the largest women's mass meeting of around 12,000. Well over 100 women's associations were founded in the early years of the movement. In 1839 stories abounded of the involvement of women in the arming and drilling occurring in the industrial districts.

Something of the spirit of the women is captured in this resolution carried by the women Chartists of Bethnal Green:

> *Woman can no longer remain in her domestic sphere, for her home has been made cheerless, her hearth comfortless, and her position degrading . . . Woman's circle has been invaded by hired bands of police ruffians – her husband dragged from her side to the gloom of a dungeon – and her children trampled under foot – and this, for no other crime than that Labour cried for its rights, and Justice for its due.*[7]

Women Chartists were also prominent in campaigns for the release of leading Chartists such as John Frost and the radical preacher, J.R. Stephens. In the 1842 strike, women were also the key to one of its most significant aspects. By 'exclusive trading' the Chartists put pressure on shopkeepers and small traders who were hostile to the movement to support the Charter, or at least to remain neutral in the battle being waged with the authorities. The middle class had benefited in terms of the vote and political rights from the reform agitation in which workers had been the driving force. Now, the Chartists reasoned, it was only just that the small property owners should support the movement to extend the suffrage to the working class.

Shopkeepers who publicly opposed the movement for the Charter were boycotted with great effect by Chartist families. Those who were supporters of the Charter were issued with licences that identified them as such. Here we can see the beginnings of a conscious grasp of the social character of the movement. Workers were using their collective strength and organisation beyond the workplace. This was no mere consumer boycott. Workers were beginning to sense and to understand their power as workers, over and above the struggle for purely formal political equality.

After one week the strike was becoming national with reports of turnouts occurring in Glasgow and the Scottish coalfields, in the industrial heartlands of England and in South Wales. Manchester, however, remained the storm centre. It was at Manchester too that a national leadership began to emerge under the momentum of the strike itself.

The Great Delegate Conference

Trades conferences were being organised to take stock of the situation and to attempt to co-ordinate the movement. On 9 August the power-loom workers met. The following day a conference of millwrights, mechanics, moulders, smiths and engineers took place, called, it is thought, by the workers of Sharp, Roberts & Co., then the largest factory in the world. This conference was reconvened the following day after it was attacked by troops. The mill hands met separately on 11 August, but by now the trades were converging as the call went out for a general delegate conference of all trades to be held on 15 August. To this end, dozens of meetings were called across the city and in the surrounding towns. Time and again the Charter was proclaimed as the only means of satisfying the demands of the workers once and for all.

The Great Delegate Conference marked a watershed in the general strike of 1842. Not only had a national leadership emerged under the direct delegated control of the strikers themselves, but the political aspect of the strike and the economic demands which had triggered it were now to lock powerfully together. At the head of the strike movement, leaders of national stature such as Peter McDouall and Richard Pilling, who understood the revolutionary potential of the situation, had also come to prominence.

The delegates were impatient of anything which smacked of a lack of seriousness. In response to a suggestion by a handful of delegates that the names of those present should not be made public in case of victimisation by employers, the chairman retorted sharply that 'those who were under any feelings of dread had better retire from the room because the time was come when every man must act honestly, openly and with a final determination (Cheers)'.[8]

Crowds were gathering outside the conference, despite magistrates' orders that they should disperse, as the delegates inside rose to give their reports from the localities. Again and again it was stated that the view of workers of all the trades was that the aim of the strike must be political change. Motions calling for the struggle to be limited to wages alone were overwhelmingly rejected. In the words of one of the delegates, 'Political rights are imperatively necessary for the preservation of our wages.'[9] The conference voted overwhelmingly for the adoption of the Charter.

Chartism had always had a mass working-class base; indeed, had emerged out of a mass working-class movement. But what had occurred at the Manchester conference was something qualitatively new. Up to this point Chartism and organisation within the trades, while they had overlapped in terms of the issues they addressed, and very often in terms of the individual activists involved, had run somewhat parallel to each other. Through the general strike and the Great Delegate Conference, Chartism had won the leadership of a now highly organised workers' movement, increasingly confident of its strength and focused on its objectives. It was this fusing of politics and economic demands which terrified the ruling class. The Home Secretary of the conservative Peel government, Sir James Graham, could see the danger the Manchester conference posed to the establishment:

> It is quite clear that these Delegates . . . are the Directing Body;
> they form the link between the Trade Unions and the Chartists,
> and a blow struck at this Confederacy goes to the heart of the evil,
> and cuts off its ramifications.[10]

The executive of the NCA had met on 16 August and, very much under McDouall's initiative, had pledged to support the strike and called for its extension across the country. Graham now resolved to strike hard at this newly emerged leadership. Already troops and police had been marching back and forth outside the conference in an attempt to intimidate those inside. Orders were now addressed to Manchester magistrates to arrest delegates. Soon a number of the most important leaders were behind bars and leadership now fell back to the localities.

Military mobilisations in the North were continuing and troops from London were being dispatched to the strike centres. But the strike had also had its effect on London workers. Mass meetings of thousands in support of the strike had already been taking place in areas where there was a tradition of Chartist organisation. As troops were assembled for embarkation, crowds gathered to oppose them. They hissed and groaned as the soldiers marched by, and called out for them not to shoot on starving workers. Confrontations occurred as workers attempted to prevent troops from boarding their trains. At Chalk Farm, crowds were charged with bayonets to clear the way for the soldiers. This opposition did have some effect. One report tells of 30 soldiers being marched in leg irons to the Tower for refusing to fire on the crowds.

As the strike continued to spread, despite harassment by the state, it was the very orderliness and level of organisation that the authorities found so difficult to handle. The turn-outs were not the wild 'mobs' the press of the time chose to describe them as. They did not, for example, indulge in looting every property they came across, which, considering the numbers in which they marched, they clearly had the power to do. They certainly relied on sympathetic storekeepers to provide them with bread and drink on their way. Reports of ransacking or theft, however, are very few and far between. On some occasions, strikers who were all for taking what they could get were scolded sharply by the rest and pulled away lest such behaviour detract from their cause.

There was real political judgement here. There was an understanding that, while the momentum of the strike was totally under the control of the workers themselves, nonetheless to alienate the small traders and shopkeepers, who were a part of the industrial communities, would be to drive them into the arms of the state and potentially into becoming recruits for the yeomanry. Secondly, there was the question of political clarity in the appeal for other workers to turn out. The very strength of the strike call was that this was not simply yet another battle for immediate material improvement, whether of wages or of loot, desperate though the strikers were. Rather this was a decisive confrontation – a challenge to the state – through which to remedy the workers' conditions for good. Any actions that clouded this argument were seen as a danger for the strike and undermining its appeal to workers of all trades to join.

This same level of class consciousness which had come to characterise the strike was also seen in the actions of the strike committees, or 'committees of public safety' as they were initially called, which operated in the localities. Temporary exemptions were granted to employers either on humanitarian grounds or where valuable materials were likely to spoil if their processing was not completed or where machinery was at risk if not closed down properly. In such cases a licence carrying the seal of the strike committee would be issued to the employer in question. In one case at Stalybridge, a master tailor was given permission to complete a funeral order. In another case, coal was provided for an engine which prevented a mineshaft from flooding.

None of this should be taken as evidence that the strikers had any illusions whatever about the large employers. Indeed, a debate had gone on within the Chartist movement on this question with respect to the Anti-Corn Law League. This was an alliance of manufacturers who opposed the government specifically on the matter of the tax on bread, which was keeping the price high. The League repeatedly made overtures to the Chartists and sections of the working class movement for a united campaign. Indeed, a section of the movement saw this as the way forward. The CSU, for example, broke away on just this question. In the main, however, the Chartists were vehemently opposed to such an alliance.

The real issue for the manufacturers was their desire to reduce wages. As Engels was to put it:

> the long and the short of the matter is this: the Corn Laws keep the price of bread higher than in other countries, and thus raise wages; but these high wages render difficult competition of the manufacturers against other nations in which bread, and consequently wages, are cheaper. The Corn Laws being repealed, the price of bread falls, and wages gradually approach those of other European countries . . .[11]

This had now been clearly exposed. The savage wage reductions that had triggered the strike to begin with had come from the very Anti-Corn Law employers who had posed as friends of the workers. Even before the strike, conference delegates had reported again and again that the workers they represented wanted nothing to do with the League. The aim was the Charter and nothing but the Charter.

The end of the strike

While the strike retained its political focus, its momentum also grew. With the smashing of the Manchester conference, however, and the removal of a national leadership, the character of the strike began to change. As the leadership fell more and more to the localities, wages became the predominant issue. While the Charter remained the banner under which the strikers marched, on a practical level it could hardly be achieved on an area-by-area basis. Wages, however, could be fought over locally. There was also evidence of employers in some regions making concessions to the strike on the wage front. This, plus the continuing repression and arrests taking place around the country, meant that the strike began to falter.

During the third week, the strikers were still resilient. There were reports of some owners opening their mills in expectation of a return to work, only having to close them again when the numbers of workers who appeared for work were so small that it was considered uneconomical to start production. By the fourth week, however, some areas were beginning to settle with employers. Still the strike did not simply collapse. The Lancashire weavers, for example, were not alone in staying out till the seventh week.

Arrests were taking place all over the country on a mass scale. In the North West alone, 1,500 were brought to trial. The sentences were harsh. Over 200 Chartists were transported to Australia and Tasmania to be little more than slaves.

One trial, however, that of Feargus O'Connor and 58 other defendants, was postponed until March of the following year. Over the intervening months, a distinct shift had occurred in the attitude of a section of the ruling class towards the working-class movement. A more conciliatory tone prevailed. A new bourgeois consciousness was emerging which was beginning to understand the immense potential power of industrial labour.

This new class of industrial workers was here to stay. It was clearly going to grow both in numbers and in organisation. State repression, rule by force alone, had proved to be a dangerous policy. Over a period of decades, it had created conditions in which revolutionary outbursts by workers had severely rocked the established order. It was a policy that simply did not provide a stable social framework for the normal maintenance of production and profits. A new and more sophisticated policy began to develop among the more far-sighted manufacturers of the time. If the workers' movement could not be suppressed then it had, in part, to be co-opted into the mainstream of the country's political institutions. The key to this strategy was for a new dialogue to be built between the state and the leadership of the working class.

The trial of 1843 was marked by an absence of the ruling-class viciousness that had typified previous trials. The defendants had been out on bail since the postponement of the case. The proceedings were low key and conducted without the full glare of publicity. This was not a show trial designed to intimidate. Thirty-eight of the defendants were sentenced to terms of imprisonment. The prosecution's case, however, fell on a 'technicality' and all were released. The government, not previously known for its fastidiousness on questions of legal detail, chose not to institute a further trial.

Here, then, was the seed for a new form of capitalist rule, one that was based on conciliation and, where it was both possible and expedient, on concession. It was a strategy that the ruling class was forced to develop and refine in response to working-class resistance over the following century.

After the defeat of the 1842 strike, an interlude of six years occurred before the next outbreak of active Chartism. In these years, the Chartist movement developed in different directions as it sought to sustain itself in circumstances of a lower level of struggle. We will follow the most important of these strands as well as taking the opportunity to reflect on the more general aspects of Chartism.

Never Give Up

Never give up! it is wiser and better
Always to hope than once to despair;
Fling off the load of Doubt's cankering fetter,
And break the dark spell of tyrannical care;
Never give up! or the burden may sink you –
Providence kindly has mingled the cup,
And, in all trials or troubles, bethink you,
The watchword of life must be, Never give up!

Never give up! there are chances and changes
Helping the hopeful a hundred to one,
And through the chaos High Wisdom arranges
Ever success – if you'll only hope on:
Never give up! For the wildest is boldest,
Knowing that providence mingles the cup;
And of all maxims the best, as the oldest
Is the true watchword of Never give up!

Never give up! – tho' the grape shot may rattle,
Or the full thunder-cloud over you burst,
Stand like a rock, – and the storm or the battle
Little shall harm you, though doing their worst:
Never give up! if adversity presses,
Providence wisely has mingled the cup,
And the best counsel, in all your distresses,
Is the stout watchword of Never give up!

Northern Star, 22 February 1845

Chapter 4   The years of drift: 1842–1848

The Land Plan

The General Strike of 1842 had, for a time, eclipsed tensions within the Chartist movement. In the period following 1842, however, the contradictory nature of Chartism became more apparent than at any other time. The divergent tendencies which had begun to emerge after the Newport uprising were now breaking forth with a new vigour. Between 1842 and 1848 we see not only the most dramatically progressive and revolutionary aspects of the movement displayed, but also the more utopian, backward-looking and, in a historical sense, even reactionary elements developing in opposition. It is at this stage of the Chartists' history that it is most true to say that Chartism anticipated every future development of the working-class movement over the next century and a half.

Certainly, the most ambitious departure from what had been the main aim of achieving the Charter, both in the scale of its conception and in actual implementation, was the Land Plan. The plan was the brainchild of Feargus O'Connor, who had become by this stage the unquestioned and adored leader of Chartism. The Land Plan was to dominate the activities and debates of the movement from the NCA Convention of 1843, when it was first taken up for consideration, till its suppression by Act of Parliament in 1851.

O'Connor's idea was simple. Workers would be settled on their own 4-acre plots of land. Subscriptions to the scheme were to be invited and the allocation of plots was to be decided by ballot. Each subscriber who was drawn in the ballot would receive a sum of money enabling them to purchase stock and equipment. Finally, collective settlements were to be established wherein the landholders could pool their energies and resources for the good of all.

The inspiration for the idea of land settlement drew to some extent on the experience of the Owenite movement. Robert Owen was a representative of a radicalised rationalism that became widely influential within the working-class movement. Appalled at the degree of poverty and social polarisation that he saw, Owen proselytised the virtues of communal life. He founded a number of

*Feargus O'Connor:
architect of the
Chartist Land Plan*

communities in England and America. Owen eventually became frustrated with the imperviousness of the governments of the day to his enlightened social philosophy. For a brief period in the early 1830s, he looked to the newly emerging trade union movement to achieve his vision. Owenism as a movement continued after Owen's death and survived as a current within the working-class movement through the Chartist years. O'Connor's Land Plan and the Owenite utopians differed only in that the basic principle of Owenite societies was communitarian. A strong hostility to individual ownership ran through Owenism, while it was to be the foundation of O'Connor's scheme. For both, however, the primary motivation was the liberation of workers from the oppression of the industrial system. Freedom from such oppression, in O'Connor's vision, was to be realised in 'an aggregate of happy individuals, rather than in a community of a few owners of all...aggregate wealth...upon whose speculation, whim and caprice the poor man must now depend for his bread'.[1]

O'Connor's idealism and optimism for the plan knew no bounds. If those with money to invest were to do so, he proclaimed, he 'would change the whole face of society in twelve months'.[2] Indeed the plan met with huge enthusiasm from workers of the time. At its peak the Land Company, set up to administrate the scheme, enjoyed the support of 70,000 subscribers, and raised £100,000. Five settlements were established at which 250 allottees were actually settled on the land. The first was Heronsgate (later renamed O'Connorville) near Watford. This was followed by Lowbands in

Worcestershire, Minster Lovell (later renamed Charterville) in Oxfordshire, Snig's End in Gloucestershire and Great Dodford in Worcestershire. The spirit of these communities is expressed in a piece from the Chartists' newspaper, the *Northern Star*, on the occasion of a gathering at O'Connorville, attended by delegations from Yorkshire, Lancashire, Exeter and Plymouth among others:

> *On entering the gates, the Band played 'The Chartist Land March' . . . The first object that met our view, was a huge tricoloured banner floating high above an immense chestnut tree, bearing the inscription, O'Connorville; and secondly Rebecca, the Chartist Cow, like the sacred cows of old, clothed in her vesture of tricolour, rendered holy by the popular voice, which is the voice of God; next, the immense Dancing Booth, erected for the accommodation of our Chartist friends, attracting the attention of everyone. The remaining booths for refreshment and amusement, were also of a very elegant character. Several 'Wandering Minstrels' attended, and earned the patronage of the visitors by singing 'The People's First Estate'. . .*[3]

The mass working-class appeal of the Land Plan is clear when we look at the occupations of its subscribers. The greatest support came from the weavers and labourers. Other groups who invested in large numbers were shoemakers, tailors, stockingers, spinners, miners, woolcombers, smiths, lacemakers and carpenters. In fact, almost every trade imaginable is represented in the list of shareholders. This mass support for what to the modern reader seems such an unlikely and utopian notion may be difficult to comprehend. In historical context, however, the popularity of the plan is not hard to grasp.

The first thing to say about the scheme is that in the Britain of the 1840s the idea of obtaining a small plot of land and making it viable as a means of sustenance was not completely fanciful. Commentators of the time, for example, reported the commercial success of allotment holders working on as little as one quarter of an acre of land.[4] But this does not explain the financial support of tens of thousands of workers who had only a slim chance of actually obtaining a plot and whose poverty hardly allowed them to be frivolous with their money. Such mass support can, in the end, only be explained by the deep alienation felt by workers living in the misery and filth of the manufacturing towns.

'Fire vomits darkness, where the lime-trees grew', wrote James Leach.[5] It is probably impossible really to understand the disgust felt by the workers and artisans of the mid-nineteenth century at the environment in which they lived and worked, and by the Chartists who attempted to articulate those feelings. In Chartist lecture halls, in front of working-class audiences, a common theme of debate was 'Man versus the Machine'. At the great gathering at Peep Green, one of the resolutions passed expressed the hope that 'man may become of more value than the machine of wood, iron and stone'.[6]

The Chartists condemned the factory system for dehumanising the lives of working-class people:

> whilst the ruthless hand of the oppressor has dragged our wives
> and little ones into the factory or loathsome mine . . . the father
> and husband is an unwilling idler and a pauper, living on the
> blood and vitals of those he loves.[7]

Marx too, registering the experience of the workers' movements emerging in contemporary European society, wrote of the physical and moral degradation of working-class life under the march of industrial capitalism. Capitalism had undoubtedly dramatically accelerated the productive power of human labour. However, since workers did not control this process, the result was not a liberation of human potential but rather its subordination. The machine, then, far from representing a release from drudgery and oppression, became a dehumanising force:

> Man (the worker) only feels himself active in his animal functions
> – eating, drinking, procreating, or at most in his dwelling and in
> dressing up etc.; and in his most human functions he no longer
> feels himself to be anything but an animal. What is animal
> becomes human and what is human becomes animal.[8]

For Marx, however, it was not 'the machine' as such which was the oppressor, but rather the capitalist class system. Marx looked beyond the misery created by capitalism and saw its progressive aspect. Whilst the factory system clearly produced massive suffering for millions of workers, in raising the level of production it also provided the basis for a leap forward in social development. Capitalism was clearing away the old feudal system which had held economic and cultural life in stagnation for centuries. As it did this, it was at the same time creating a new class of industrial workers who possessed the necessary cohesion, organisation and power to overthrow capitalism and replace it with something very different. It was capitalism, in Marx's view, which had made socialism possible.

Despite the historically progressive significance of the industrial system, however, it is little wonder that for many thousands of working-class families the idea of escaping the city for the clean air of the countryside had a powerful appeal. No matter how romantic the charm of the rural idyll may have been, the idea of small land ownership represented liberation from oppression in the imagination of the nineteenth-century worker.

The same desire to flee from social distress lay behind the setting up of the emigration clubs. As unemployment spiralled upwards, leaving tens of thousands of families destitute, a life in one of the British colonies seemed to offer some hope. As William Stott, President of the Bradford Woolcombers' Society, was to put it in 1850:

> *If the mass of us are not required, then we appeal to the justice of the manufacturers and merchants to enable the able-bodied to emigrate. We ask neither pity nor compassion; we require justice.*[9]

Whatever the aspiration and promise of the Land Plan, however, the reality was somewhat different. A number of the national leaders of the Chartist movement were opposed to O'Connor's scheme. They complained, rightly, that the appeal for a return to the land was historically backward looking and, in the conditions of a rapidly industrialising economy, was actually absurd. James Bronterre O'Brien, widely recognised as the theorist of the movement and second only to Feargus O'Connor in the national leadership, called instead for the land to be nationalised for the benefit of all. Their hostility was further roused by support from elements among the Tories.

Today the idea of a working-class movement attracting support from Tories seems bizarre. However, in mid-nineteenth-century Britain there were a small number of prominent individuals who did ally themselves to working-class protest. The social basis for the Tories in the nineteenth century lay largely among the landed gentry. They were opposed to the Whig governments of the day and their identification with the expansion of manufacturing capitalism. The bulk of landowners, however, eventually accommodated to the new system. It provided them with new farming technologies through which they were able to increase their competitiveness and to intensify the exploitation of their labourers. It also provided new areas of investment for their fortunes. Indeed, no great conflict existed between their interests and those of the industrialists of the great cities.

To the social friction generated by the shift to the factory system, however, isolated individuals reacted unpredictably. The name of Richard Oastler, for example, a Yorkshire Tory, had become firmly associated with the factory reform movement. As one of its leading figures, he had even been dubbed 'The King of the Factory Children'. The Labourers' Friend Society, a Tory–Whig grouping, campaigned in the 1830s for land to be allotted to farm labourers. Its main motivation, however, was to tie land workers more closely to the large estates, increase productivity and maintain low wages.

The illusion of support from a small section of the ruling class, together with a condemnation of 'the machine' and a semi-mystical belief in the land as the worker's salvation, led O'Connor to advocate voting for Tory candidates in elections to beat the Whigs. O'Brien was beside himself with rage at this extraordinary nineteenth-century version of tactical voting:

> *Our business as Chartists is . . . to disavow both factions alike . . . What! Vote for a Tory merely to keep out a Whig! Vote for a villain who wants to put down me, and my principles, and my party, by brute force, merely to get rid of another villain who has tried the same game and failed! No! damn me if I do . . . And as to the new hocus-pocus policy of promoting Chartism by inundating the next House of Commons with Toryism, I cannot find language capable of expressing my contempt for it.*[10]

The Land Plan was ultimately a failure. Urban workers who had little or no experience of tillage or animal husbandry did not fare well on the land. Reports came in of allottees actually hiring farm labourers to perform the tasks they could not carry out themselves. The crisis in the Land Plan unfolded as accusations of financial irregularity were levelled at O'Connor. In fact, it is fairly well established today that O'Connor was not corrupt. On the contrary, his enthusiasm for and dedication to the movement were utterly sincere. However, he was no book-keeper and the scheme had suffered from bad management. Certainly, enough of the mud stuck to cause a loss of confidence on the part of investors. By the early 1850s the government had the pretext it had been looking for and a select committee was set up to investigate the Land Company and close it down.

Despite the mass support that the Land Plan had won among workers, it had never achieved sufficient scale in its implementation to represent much of a real threat to the ruling class. However, a scheme based on so loud a denunciation of the prevailing order and so contrary to the industrial expansionism of the time could not be tolerated by the authorities. But it was not merely the ideological significance of the plan which brought about its repression by the state. The Land Plan had, by the late 1840s, become something of a

Chartist flagship, representing a movement which, in its most active phases, had severely rocked nineteenth-century capitalism. It is this, more than anything else, which explains the ruling-class hatred vented in the suppression of 1851.

Methodists and teetotallers

Although the Land Plan was by far the most celebrated development from Chartism in this period, other strands of the movement were forging their own path. One such strand was 'teetotal Chartism'. Some Chartists had actually begun their political life in the temperance movement. Most, however, looked to temperance as a new direction for Chartism in the wake of the explosions of 1839 and 1842. Henry Vincent, for example, the fiery orator whose arrest had provoked the Newport uprising, came out of gaol a convinced advocate of abstinence from drink, snuff and tobacco.

The motives behind teetotal Chartism were complex. Certainly, for some the main concern was to give the Chartist movement a more respectable image and to curry favour with the middle classes. But this picture of a drunken working-class mob contrasted with a temperate middle class was something of a fallacy. A few years before, Francis Place, who took a dim view of alcohol himself, pointed out the hypocrisy:

> When a man in easy circumstances gets drunk, it is either at his own house or at the house of a friend, whence he goes home in a coach and is not exposed to the public gaze. A working man gets drunk at a public house and staggers along the streets; here he is seen by everybody, and is inconsiderately taken to be a fair representative of his class . . .[11]

George Julian Harney's response was somewhat more acidic:

> I protest against the insolence of those who dare to lecture the working classes on their 'immorality' while they themselves live by the most immoral system that this earth was ever afflicted with – a system which bases the wealth, luxuries and pleasures of the few, upon the poverty, crime and misery of the many.[12]

But moralism was not the only element in the reasoning of the teetotallers. Again, when we look at the movement in context, a rather more sympathetic picture emerges. On the one hand, the predominant culture of working-class communities, in good times, was imbued with a certain lust for living in which drink played no small part. One Trowbridge Chartist promised his audiences that the Charter would bring with it 'plenty of roast beef, plum pudding and strong beer by working three hours a day'.[13] On the other hand, drink was associated with army recruitment and with the purchasing of parliamentary seats. Over and above this, there was the feeling that drink befuddled the minds of workers as to their real interests. As one writer in the *Northern Star* put it, 'Teetotalism leads to knowledge – knowledge leads to thinking – thinking leads to discontent of things as they are, and then, as a matter of course, comes Chartism.'[14]

But it was not simply disapproval that led some Chartists to be drawn by teetotalism. Some argued that it might even be used as a weapon of struggle for democratic rights. Before the existence of a welfare state of any description, direct taxation by the government was so unpopular that it was simply not an option. State finance for the army and police came entirely from indirect taxation. In the 1840s the government raised a third of its revenue from drink taxes. Surely, then, if the majority of workers were to abstain from drink, the government would become bankrupt and be brought to its knees. The argument had a charm, and the audience for it was not inconsiderable, but it was nonetheless an essentially moral one.

To the extent that drunkenness did exist among the working class of the day, it grew directly from the oppression and misery of its condition. To expect workers to put down the bottle before changing the social conditions that led to it was putting the cart before the horse. In the words of George Bartlett, Bath shoemaker and 'moral politician', 'Men are first made poor, and then intemperate.'[15] Temperance Chartism did not survive as a national focus after the early 1840s.

A related development of the movement was religious Chartism. Like any movement, Chartism was of its day, and although during its most active phases it was a strongly secular movement, in these years of drift a number of Chartists moved towards the radical and dissenting churches.

The Christianity of the religious Chartists was Methodism. They responded to the radical egalitarianism of its message and its rejection of clerical hierarchy. This 'primitive' Methodism at points infused an almost revivalist spirit to parts of the movement. In Lancashire, Yorkshire and the Midlands, Methodist gatherings took place on the hills and moorlands of the area. Political sermons and Bible readings were given and hymns were sung with great enthusiasm. Chartist churches sprang up around the country. The seats were free, ministers were unpaid and no doctrinal obedience was demanded of the faithful. The congregations helped the unemployed, collected money for political prisoners and signed Chartist petitions. Needless to say, the established Church poured scorn on such proceedings. The vicar of St Stephens in Norwich told his flock, 'I have learned, in whatever station in life, therewith to be content.' The Chartists who were present shouted, 'You get £200 a year! Come and weave bombases.'[16]

The religious aspect of Chartism was not the most typical. But, to the extent that it was present, it reflected the peculiar historical moment that had created the movement. John Wycliffe in the late fourteenth century had poured pious venom on the heads of the idle rich. The radical movements of the seventeenth and eighteenth centuries had used the language of the Bible to voice their social protest. The Levellers had demanded equality on earth as well as in the after-life. And now, within Chartism, a movement that was carving out a new secular tradition in the working class, still one face was turned towards the traditions of the past.

The educational Chartists

Another of the 'new directions' was education. By the time John Collins and William Lovett were released from prison in 1840, they were convinced educational Chartists. Lovett had written a book with the title *Chartism: A New Organisation of the People*. What he proposed was a national system of education for the working class to be financed independently of the state by subscriptions from workers. District halls were to be built in every major industrial community for the education of children and adults.

The appeal for education clubs to be set up met with an enthusiastic response in many areas. In order to prevent state control, those who sat on the school committees had to be members of the NCA and were to be elected by universal suffrage of all adults living in the surrounding areas.

When we compare these Chartist schools with the state education that began to develop in the last quarter of the nineteenth century, the contrast is astonishing. The state's National Monitoring Schools were based on extreme regimentation, massive pupil to teacher ratios – one teacher would frequently instruct 500 children with the aid of pupil-helpers – and learning by drill. The Chartist schools of the 1840s were imbued with a rather different spirit. The most famous was at the Carpenters' Hall in Manchester. Here the principles included non-denominational acceptance of all children, which allowed Catholic children to attend, and instruction in the

William Lovett:
educational Chartist

principles of democracy and the People's Charter. The attitude of the Chartist educationalists towards the children was progressive even by modern standards:

> *no corporeal punishment or particular mark of degradation [will] be allowed to be inflicted on any of the children, for any forwardness or contrariety they may evince during their attendance at school. But instead of the cane or the whip, the more rational means be used – as entreating, mild expostulation, and kindness on the part of the conductors and teachers, shall be substituted, and strictly attended to in all cases.*[17]

Although educational Chartism captured something of the enlightenment that permeated the movement, and is inspiring for us today, it was an eddy which again moved away from the struggle for democratic rights for the working class. Lovett was firmly in the 'Moral Force' camp. He did not believe that workers were yet ready for political power. Only after a period of moral and cultural improvement would the working class achieve the necessary knowledge and responsibility to lay full claim to their political rights. The fact that the middle classes were invited to take part in this new direction for Chartism further antagonised the O'Connorites. Indeed, all those in the movement who saw the working class as being a self-liberating social class were suspicious of these new educators. O'Connor, impatient of any distraction from the main aims of the Charter, other than his own, was apoplectic:

> **National Education**. *National jackass! You may just as well talk of a national Jackass, a national pig, a national cow, or a national horse... as talk of a National Education, or anything else national, till we have a nation... There is no national character; there is the machinations of necessity, brought on by misrule upon the one hand, and the retaliation of expediency upon the other... Before you can have anything national you must first have a nation... A people must have a Charter before they can have a nation. Get the Charter, and then call England the **Great Nation**, and any court in Europe will believe you; but now they laugh at you, and call your country a **Great Workshop**.[18]*

Chartist internationalism

The new enlightenment within the working class which Chartism represented was not confined to initiatives such as those of the educationalists. It was something that pervaded the movement on many levels. One of the most remarkable aspects of the Chartist movement was its thoroughgoing internationalism. This was most apparent in the Chartists' opposition to British rule in Ireland. Many in the movement had cut their teeth in politics in activity against the Coercion Acts, which had effectively abolished political rights of association and organisation in Ireland. There was a keen understanding that, if such methods of rule could be used across the Irish Sea, then they could just as well be used against the workers of England, Scotland and Wales.

Some Chartist activity did exist in Ireland. However, the dominance of the national question in Irish radicalism meant that class politics were pushed into the background and Chartism never became a mass movement. Chartist membership, at its peak, may have approached 1,000. In Britain, however, Irish immigrant labourers were to have an enormous impact on the radicalism and energy of the movement.

In nineteenth-century British society, anti-Irish feeling ran high. This was partly the result of press and government propaganda used to justify the subjugation of the Irish. Among the working class, however, it had a more material basis. Employers commonly used Irish labourers as strike-breakers. In times of recession, unskilled Irish workers were used to undercut wages and conditions. None of this had benefited the Irish themselves. Indeed, the most destitute of any of the industrial workers were always the Irish. In 1841 in Lancashire, 70 per cent of juvenile offenders were of Irish parentage.[19]

Thus English and Irish workers were pitted against each other in competition to the detriment of both. Only as a consequence of a great mass movement such as the Chartists, which drew English and Irish workers together, could anti-Irish racism be overcome. This was reflected in the strong Irish representation in the leadership. It was also reflected in the huge involvement of Irish workers in the Chartist and trade union movements. As one employer, giving evidence before a parliamentary commission, put it:

> Where there is discontent, or a disposition to combine, or turn-outs among the work people, the Irish are the leaders; they are the most difficult to reason with and convince on the subject of wages and regulations in the factories.[20]

Irish workers had brought their own forms of radicalism into England. In Ireland the Ribbon movement, for example, an agrarian combination movement, had gained a strong footing. Now the Ribbonists who had emigrated to England took up their organisation again. It was no coincidence that, where this semi-clandestine movement was strong, so too was Chartism and the Irish influence within it.

The Chartists, however, did not take Irish involvement in the movement for granted. Conscious efforts were made both to enlist the support of Irish workers and to educate English workers as to the oppression of Ireland and the Irish. The *Northern Star* ran articles on aspects of life in Ireland. The demand for the repeal of the Act of Union between Britain and Ireland was included in the Chartist petition of 1842. Indeed, there was considerable cooperation between Chartists and repeal agitators. In 1844 John West of Halifax reported:

> The Irish Repealers and the Chartists are on the best of terms. The Repealers regularly attend the Chartist meetings, and in turn the Chartists do all in their power to aid and assist them. I had a good meeting at night . . . a petition of the Repealers which was in the room was signed by everyone present . . .[21]

The link was also made in the street ballads of the time, such as that about the 'Gagging Act' of 1848:

> Now you must look before you speak
> And mind what you are after,

'Tis death if you should say 'Repeal',
Or, 'please we want the Charter'.
Sew up your mouths without delay,
The government proposes,
And what the people wants to say
Must whistle through their noses.[22]

When agitation for Irish independence was renewed in Ireland in 1843, the Chartists organised demonstrations and rallies in support. At every turn the message was clear. As Marx was to put it, while English workers did not support the struggle for Irish independence, they would never themselves be free.

Chartist internationalism did not stop at the Irish question. The continental independence and revolutionary movements were also a source of fascination and solidarity. The Chartists were inspired by the struggle for Hungarian independence. The *Northern Star* reported on a resolution that was passed at a meeting for Hungary held in City Hall of Glasgow:

> *That this meeting regards with deep emotion the heroic struggles of the people of Hungary in defence of the right of self-government, and deems their resistance to Austrian oppression just and worthy of the sympathy of the people of Great Britain, while it views with horror the atrocities to which the Hungarians have been subjected. This meeting pledges itself to use every available means to prevent further excesses against that people by the barbarous governments of Austria and Russia.* [23]

When General Heynau, the Austrian butcher of the 1848 revolutions, came to visit a brewery, he was physically attacked by the brewery workers and had to flee for his life. The women workers 'tore the fellow's grisly mustachios until he roared again and again with pain and fury'.[24] The visits of other European tyrants, such as Louis-Philippe of France and Tsar Nicholas, were occasions of protests by Chartists and the émigré groups that peppered the London political scene.

The Canadian and Polish independence movements produced a similar response in England to that of the Hungarian movement. When the Cracow uprising occurred, the manifesto of the Cracow free state was translated into English. Public meetings were held to raise awareness of the Polish struggle, and leaflets were circulated calling on the British government to refrain from intervention on the side of the Austrian oppressors.

Recognition of the identity of interests between the British working class and the oppressed peoples of the colonies is well captured by O'Brien who, in a passage laced with irony, replies to a fictitious Whig on the question of whether Chartists would fight to defend the colonies:

> *Let all those who have possessions in India, or all who profit by what you call 'our Indian possessions' be off to India, and fight a thousand battles for them if they like . . . and all such other aristocrats and commercial speculators as have either wrung or are now wringing, fortunes out of Hindoo sweat and misery – let all such persons go and fight for our 'Indian possessions', but let them not mock our degradation by asking us, working people to fight alongside them, either for our 'possessions' in India, or anywhere else, seeing that we do not possess a single acre of ground, or any description of property in our own country, much less colonies, or 'possessions' in any other, having been robbed of everything we ever earned by the middle and upper classes.*[25]

Within this spirit of internationalism, a profound anti-racism also flourished. The Chartists opposed slavery and supported the abolitionist movement. As the Catholic Chartists of Bradford put it, 'all are included in the Charter, without distinction of party, sect or colour'.[26] The most prominent London leader, William Cuffay, was himself black – the son of a slave from St Kitts. *The Times* had mocked the London Chartists as 'the black man and his party' and, at the time of Cuffay's trial and eventual transportation to Tasmania where he died at the age of 82, called him 'half a nigger'. His own movement saw him differently:

> *Whilst integrity in the midst of poverty, whilst honour in the midst of temptation are admired and venerated, so long will the name of William Cuffay, a scion of Africa's oppressed race, be preserved from oblivion.*[27]

The internationalism of Chartism was the product of the sharpest class struggles that had ever occurred in British society between industrial workers and capitalists. These struggles had thrown into clear relief the identity of interests amongst the workers and oppressed of all countries and races. After the great confrontations of 1839 and 1842 had passed, however, this clarity had begun to fade.

The trade union question

The drift of the mid-1840s was not merely one of a lack of direction. A new strategy was emerging – a strategy of gradualism and reliance on the support of the middle class. The seeds of a new reformism were being sown. Even if overthrowing the rule of the rich now seemed less of a possibility, it might still be possible to achieve some kind of accommodation within the system – or so the argument went. A recovery in trade also lent itself to the idea that trade union action alone might bring some improvement in wages and conditions.

This move away from the political focus of the Charter was met with distrust by many among the Chartist leadership, including O'Connor. The trade union struggle was seen as being ultimately futile. Even if a temporary improvement in wages and working conditions was achieved, the rapid boom–slump cycles of the nineteenth century meant that these gains would be quickly taken away. 'Strikes always fail' became something of a slogan of the time.

The Chartists could not, however, ignore the trades organisations for long. A number of the most important trade union leaders, such as John Doherty of the cotton spinners, and William Cuffay and John Parker in the London movement, were themselves Chartists or were close to Chartism. On top of this, by the mid-1840s many of the workers' organisations were becoming increasingly politicised in the course of their struggles. Some began to sponsor the Land Plan and cooperative schemes. While some sections of the movement continued to look to conciliation with the employers in the form, for example, of the National Association of United Trades, others declared their support for the Charter. When the national associations of the shoemakers and tailors were set up, Chartists and Owenites were given prominent positions. In 1844 Chartists and the trade unions were involved in joint activity against extending the Masters and Servants legislation, under which workers, already legally bound to their employers, would face enormous fines for breaking their contract. Around the same time the idea of striking for the Charter was being floated once again.

There were leading Chartists, such as Bronterre O'Brien and Peter Murray McDouall, who understood the significance of the rise of workers' organisations. While it may have been true that the outlook of the unions was by and large more conservative than that of the Chartists, the fact remained that they represented something very significant. Through trade union organisation, workers were beginning to understand their power, not only to fight to improve their conditions, but also to achieve political change.

But even those Chartists who were most closely associated with the trade unions did not fully grasp the relationship between the economic struggles of the working class and its political aspect. They certainly understood the importance of giving the trade union struggle a political focus in the Charter. But the Charter was still, in a sense, elevated above the movement, the trade unions being, perhaps, its vehicle. What was missing was a grasp of the dynamic between these two sides of the class struggle. Rosa Luxemburg, writing over half a century later in a rather different context, addressed the question brilliantly:

> The movement does not go only in one direction, from an economic to a political struggle, but also in the opposite direction . . . With the spread, clarification and intensification of the political struggle not only does the economic struggle not recede, but on the contrary it spreads and at the same time becomes more organised and intensified. There exists a reciprocal influence between the two struggles . . . In a word, the economic struggle is the factor that advances the movement from one political focal point to another. The political struggle periodically fertilises the ground for the economic struggle. Cause and effect interchange every second.[28]

Thus the trade unionism of the 1840s was not simply a retreat from the Charter. Rather, the struggle for the Charter had actually tilled the ground from which the trades organisations now grew. In turn, the struggle for better wages and conditions, far from being subordinate to the fight for political change, would create the conditions to take it further.

The Patriot's Grave (written to the Irish martyrs)

There is blood on the earth – 'tis the blood of the brave
Who have gone to their rest to the freeman's grave!
They are dead – but the spirit they kindled is here,
With the fire breath of life, all unquenched and clear,
And strong in its might as the storm at night,
When it whirls the clouds o'er the moon so bright!

There is blood on the earth! all wild and red
It cries to our God from the freeman's bed!
It will not fade, nor be washed away
And the echoes are rife with this mournful lay.
'By gilt and wrong, both reckless and strong,
They were slain for the truth which they loved so long!'

There is blood on the earth – in vale and glen
It has water'd the flowers like dew – and men
Of the noblest heart and most fiery brain,
Have fallen, like Gods, immortal though slain;
For with death at their side, they have life for a bride
Whose beauty shall flourish whilst time betide.

Northern Star, 9 September 1843

Chapter 5   The final confrontation: 1848

Revolution in the air

For the six years from 1842, the Chartist movement had drifted with little effective direction or progress towards its aims. The movement had splintered into various fragments, some more eccentric than others. Its leadership had also factionalised over questions of principle and personality. The year 1848, however, was to mark a turning point that revived the fortunes of the movement, re-awoken by the European revolutions of that year.

The events of 1848 in Britain can only be understood in their international setting. The influence of two countries in particular – Ireland and France – converged to fill the sails of Chartism once again.

By 1848 the Irish poor had suffered three years of one of the most savage famines in history. Extortionate rents imposed by English landlords had not only forced millions of peasants into destitution, but had changed farming practice. Good land had been turned over almost exclusively to cash crop farming to pay rents and taxes. The land that was left for subsistence crops on a peasant holding was usually so poor in quality that little could be grown on it – except for potatoes. When a new strain of potato-infecting fungus arrived, the effect was devastating. The entire Irish national potato crop was destroyed and the population starved. It was not that there was no food in Ireland. Quite the contrary. The wheat harvests since 1845 had been very good. But the wheat crop was for export to England and under no circumstances, on the orders of Charles Trevelyan, head of the British treasury, was it to be used for famine relief lest it destabilise the price.

Ireland's population dropped from 8 million before the famine to 5½ million by the time of the 1851 census. One and a half million had died of famine and disease. A million more had emigrated. Many of these were to perish in their efforts to reach America.

The responsibility of the British for the misery inflicted on the Irish peasantry was not lost in Ireland itself. Riots took place in the port towns to prevent the export of wheat to England, and agrarian

Victims of the Irish famine drew support from English radicals

unrest rose to dangerous levels. Attacks on the property of landlords rose dramatically, as did attacks on landlords themselves.

The increasing levels of social tension are reflected in the crime figures of the time. In Ireland, with its small and rapidly decreasing population, recorded incidents of riot and breach of the peace rose to 3,222 for 1848 as compared with 387 in Britain. Incidents of the crimes of refusing to aid the police and rescuing those arrested stood at 4,131 compared to 9 for the whole of England and Wales. Similarly, the figures for those appearing before the courts reached record levels – 50 per cent higher than for the rest of the British Isles in 1849.[1] Between 1846 and 1847 the crimes of attempted murder by shooting, robberies of arms and firing into dwellings had all more than doubled.

As the level of social and political tension mounted, the British ruling class became increasingly alarmed at the prospect of large-scale rebellion. Towards the end of 1847, thousands of troops were sent to Ireland in anticipation of serious conflict. Anxiety within ruling circles was also reflected in the rabid anti-Irish racism of the British press. *The Times* editorialised against the uncivilised hordes across the Irish Sea. In the cartoons by Tenniel in *Punch*, the Irish were portrayed as club-wielding, ape-like creatures driven by nothing but bloodlust.

It was not only the prospect of revolt in Ireland that so worried the British ruling class. The emigration of thousands of displaced Irish to the industrial towns of England was swelling what was seen to be an already insurgent Irish population at home. News of the horror of the famine electrified the Irish communities in Britain as well as Chartist workers.

Most worrying of all for the authorities of the day, however, was the growing identification of the movement for Irish independence and the Chartist movement with one another. In Ireland itself the death in 1847 of Daniel O'Connell, the leader of the Irish Repeal Movement who had been vehemently opposed to any fraternisation with the Chartists, removed a major obstacle to unity across the Irish Sea. But more than this, the depth of the crisis in Ireland meant that the movement for freedom from British rule was itself changing. The politics of pure nationalism simply did not fit in a situation where the poor had no food to eat. The newly formed Irish Confederates now sought unity with the Chartists and enthusiastic joint meetings took place in Dublin.

In England, too, concern with the Irish issue reached a new peak. Irish Confederates spoke on Chartist platforms. Calls for solidarity with the Irish became a hallmark of Chartist meetings and rallies. One Irish speaker, addressing a meeting at Oldham Edge, asked his audience if he could go back to Ireland and say that 'if a charge of cavalry were made along the streets of Dublin, . . . half a million of men in Lancashire had sworn fealty to Ireland'. The crowd cried back, 'Yes!' One voice, referring to Feargus O'Connor, boomed, 'Tell them that an Irishman is our father in England.' The speaker continued that he spoke on behalf of the Irish people when he proclaimed, 'The Charter, the whole Charter and nothing but the Charter.' He enquired of the crowd, would they equally proclaim, 'Ireland, all Ireland and nothing but Ireland for the Irish!' Again the reply came back, 'Yes', accompanied by applause.[2]

The Chartists were very clear in the internationalism of their support for Irish independence. They understood that an uprising in Ireland would weaken the British state at home, and in so doing would put pressure on the government to concede the Charter. Equally, a successful Chartist movement would bring freedom from British rule closer for the Irish. This principle of solidarity across national borders was to be reiterated again and again as the European revolutions of 1848 unfolded.

In France, as in the rest of Europe, the cyclical crisis in the economy was creating the conditions for social explosion. Bankruptcies and financial collapse were the order of the day. The general crisis in the economy also had its effect in agriculture, producing food shortages in large areas of the country. The potato blight which had wreaked such devastation in Ireland struck on the continent as well.

The widespread sense of grievance throughout France was to find a powerful political focus in opposition to the monarchy of Louis-Philippe. Illusions that Louis-Philippe would be a reforming monarch, bringing civil liberties and democracy, had been shattered. Instead the regime had repressed political rights by such actions as taking away the freedom of the press. Revolts and conflicts with the authorities had already occurred in the rural areas. Now, however, the stage was set for something bigger.

The event which sparked the revolution was the shooting down of a crowd outside the Ministry of Foreign Affairs on 23 February. At the head of the revolution stood a left-liberal provisional government led by Alexander Ledru-Rollin, representing a capitalist class who had become impatient of the repressive regime of Louis-Philippe. The real driving force behind the revolution, however, was a working class who took to the barricades and whose outlook was distinctly socialist, albeit in varying hues. This newly conscious working class wanted to go much further than the national leaders of the revolution were prepared to contemplate. By summer 1848 this leadership was to turn ferociously on the working class to smash the challenge it represented.

The suddenness of the February revolution and the speed with which it proceeded amazed onlookers abroad. The monarchy of Louis-Philippe was swept aside. A democratic franchise was introduced. Slavery was abolished. There were even the beginnings of an attempt to solve the problem of unemployment.

The impact of the February revolution on the British ruling class, and the fear it inspired, cannot be overstated. Britain and France, separated by only 21 miles of Channel, had long been rivals. The prospect of the export of French radicalism to English shores was terrifying to them. France was, after all, a superpower, exerting profound economic, political and cultural influence across the continent. Indeed the February revolution was to inspire revolt against the regimes of old Europe, making 1848 the most truly revolutionary year of the nineteenth century.

The response to news of the February revolution in Ireland was one of heady enthusiasm. *The Freeman's Journal*, not known for its inflammatory tone among the nationalist press, ended its editorial of Monday, 28 February by proclaiming, 'Honour to the Brave Citizenry of Paris. Success to the Cause of the People'.

If the nationalists in Ireland were excited by the news from France, the Chartists in Britain were ecstatic. The news of the abdication of Louis-Philippe found the Fraternal Democrats – a grouping on the far left of the Chartist movement to which many of the European émigrés had gravitated – meeting at the White Hart tavern in Drury Lane. The report of an eyewitness who was present gives a flavour of the impact the news had:

> *The effect was electrical. Frenchmen, Germans, Poles, Magyars, sprang to their feet, embraced, shouted, and gesticulated in the*

wildest enthusiasm. Snatches of oratory were delivered in excited tones, and flags were caught from the walls, to be waved exultantly, amidst cries of 'Hoch! Eljen! Vive la Republique!' Then the doors were opened, and the whole assemblage . . . with linked arms and colours flying, marched to the meeting place of the Westminster Chartists in Dean Street, Soho. There another enthusiastic fraternisation took place, and great was the clinking of glasses that night in and around Soho and Leicester Square.[3]

All around the country, meetings in rooms, on open moors and on hillsides celebrated the new dawn of democracy in Europe. Massive rallies cheered speaker after speaker who greeted the revolution in France. Resolutions were passed and addresses sent to the people of France, in more or less flowery prose. The Salford Chartists called on the French to be a 'polar star for the guidance of surrounding nations'. Perhaps the prize for the grand romantic weep should go to the authors of the Chartist placard that appeared in Lancashire and Cheshire, which proclaimed that the revolutionaries of the European nations were 'struggling with manly vigour to rescue the fair but weeping form of liberty from the foul embrace of usurping faction'.[4]

What was clear was that after years of drift the Chartist movement was in the ascendant once again. For many in the Chartist leadership, the February revolution was a rallying call to which Chartism must rise. From the pages of the *Northern Star*, Harney cried:

How long, Men of Great Britain and Ireland, how long will you carry the damning stigma of being the only people in Europe who dare not will their freedom? Patience! The hour is nigh! From the hill-tops of Lancashire, from the voices of hundreds of thousands has ascended to Heaven the oath of union, and the rallying cry of conflict. Englishmen and Irishmen have sworn to have THE CHARTER AND REPEAL OR VIVE LA REPUBLIQUE![5]

If events in France had re-awoken the Chartist movement, events in Britain soon began to take on a momentum of their own. In every major centre the crisis in the economy was throwing thousands into the ranks of the unemployed. The winter of 1847–48 had been a severe one. The *Northern Star* reported the extreme prevalence of influenza, bronchitis, pneumonia, typhus, measles and scarlatina. Smallpox was also widespread. One diarist of the time wrote: 'Remarkable depression in the last months of this year in society; general illness; great mortality; innumerable failures . . . want of money . . . a curious presage of the impending storm.'[6]

March 1848 saw rioting around the country. In Glasgow serious clashes occurred with the authorities. Mass meetings of the unemployed had been taking place in the city, addressed particularly by McDouall. The clashes began when the 'grand break-out' took place. The bakeries were looted for bread. The gunsmiths were looted for arms. In response, the cavalry were called out and the Riot Act was read. Troops then fired into the crowd, leaving three injured and two dead. One of the corpses was later wheeled through the city streets to show what had been done.

Disturbances also took place in Edinburgh, Manchester and Oldham. The most celebrated clashes occurred in London. A demonstration at Trafalgar Square, called against a proposed rise in income tax, was turned into a democratic rally despite attempts to ban it by the authorities. Police were sent in to break up the assembly, which numbered thousands, on the pretext of a skirmish in the crowd. As Reginald Gammage, the first historian of Chartism, later recorded:

> *Some well fed sons of the favoured class got remarking on the idleness of the persons attending the meeting. This levity exasperated the parties attacked and excitement ran rather high. This formed a pretext for the police, who attempted violently to disperse the crowd, and in doing so, exercised no little amount of brutality. The people attempted a defence, and drove the police back to their quarters; but that force receiving large additions from all quarters, the people were ultimately conquered and many of them taken wounded to the hospital. In the evening, however, a large number again rallied amid cries of 'To the Palace!' and in the direction of Buckingham Palace they proceeded.*[7]

The result was running street battles between the police and sections of the crowd. What most marked the events was the astonishing amount of glass that was broken that night as lamps and shop fronts were smashed. One doctor quickly arranged his red, clear and blue medicinal bottles to represent the flag of the new French republic. The subtlety of the appeal was, unfortunately for the doctor, lost on the crowd. It is little wonder, perhaps, that orders were later given that no more loose granite was to be laid around Westminster. The London disturbances were also remembered for the extreme youth of those involved. At one point the police seized what they took to be a ringleader of the affray, judging by the epaulettes he wore upon his coat. As he was arrested, this dangerous incendiary began to cry.

Demonstrations were now taking place from Liverpool to Aberdeen. Mass Chartist gatherings were once again being organised in Macclesfield, Leeds, Oldham, Sheffield and elsewhere. A third Chartist petition had been launched which was to be presented to Parliament on 10 April. A Chartist gathering of perhaps 15,000 had already taken place at Kennington Common on 15 March, which had resulted in clashes with police.

Establishment panic

Four thousand police had been deployed against the Kennington Common assembly, and gunsmiths had been ordered to unscrew the barrels of their stock. All public buildings including the Bank of England and Buckingham Palace had been fortified. Troops were also assembled. The Home Office had taken control of security arrangements for the whole country. Ruling circles in Britain were now seriously worried about what was afoot in the country.

Expectation of some major confrontation on all sides began to mount with the calling of the Chartist Convention in London on 4 April. Lord Campbell wrote to his brother, 'This may be the last time I write to you before the Republic is established.'[8] The wife of Colonel Phipps, adviser to Prince Albert, was sure that the Chartists would 'massacre' her husband. Lady Charlotte Guest, the wife of the biggest iron founder in South Wales, was worried about the blood that would be spilled when 'the starving met the troops' and the 'implacable hate' that would result.[9] On 8 April, Waterloo station was closed to the public and several hundred special constables were stationed in order to evacuate Queen Victoria and the Royal Family to the Isle of Wight. Some were worried that even these arrangements were not secure enough. As Foreign Secretary Lord Palmerston pointed out, 'the Solent Sea is not impassable'.[10]

There was indeed plenty in what some of the Chartist leadership were saying that gave property owners cause for alarm. In late March, Ernest Jones, the Chartist socialist who was later to gain a dominating influence in the movement, addressed a meeting of the Literary Institute in London. Arguing against the moral force Chartists, he said:

> Let them look at it and say in their minds: 'You naughty wall, you ought to be lying low, why don't you tumble down'. Do you think that will clear the road. No! But if their 'power of mind' tells them to take a pick axe, and a mallet, and a crowbar, and beat the rotten barrier to atoms, then the highway to liberty will be clear.[11]

There were those amongst the Chartist leaders who were a good deal more direct than this. Figures such as William Cuffay and Charles McCarthy, representing a new, more militant leadership that was emerging as the crisis unfolded, advocated the setting up of rifle clubs. In fact, Jones himself, speaking the day before the presentation of the petition to Parliament concerning the possibility of a government attack on the Chartist Convention, claimed:

If the Government touch one hair of the head of the delegates – if they place them under arrest, or attempt the least interference with their liberty – every town represented by the delegates, would be in arms in less than twenty four hours [tremendous cheers]. If I were to be killed, or wounded, or arrested, the moment the intelligence arrived at Halifax the people would rise and disarm the troops, imprison the authorities – and 100,000 Yorkshiremen would march upon London [enthusiastic cheers]. So help me God I will march in the first rank tomorrow, and if they attempt any violence, they shall not be 24 hours longer in the House of Commons.[12]

It was this sort of rhetoric, reported in sensationalist terms by the press, which so unnerved respectable society. The Chartists were to gather on 10 April to present the third petition. This was widely held to be the day that the working class would make its bid for power. Certainly the government prepared for the worst. A Security Bill was raced through the House, and the Duke of Wellington was brought out of retirement and given military command of London.

The more tactically minded among the ruling circles were anxious to avoid another Peterloo. They had taken note of how, in France, it had been the shooting down of demonstrators which had provoked full-scale revolution less than two months before. On the day itself the troops were to be kept out of sight, in reserve. If it came to it, however, the authorities were committed to putting the Chartists down in blood. In the words of Lord Malmesbury, if resistance was offered by the Chartists, 'then the troops are instantly to appear, and the cannon to open with shell and grenades, infantry and cavalry are to charge – in short they are to be made an example of'.[13]

Eight thousand troops had been stationed along the Thames Embankment. Twelve guns had been put in place at the Royal Mews. Three steamboats stood ready for troop movements along the river. Four thousand policemen guarded the bridges, Palace Yard and Trafalgar Square. The Chelsea Pensioners had been mobilised. Most significantly, 150,000 special constables were sworn in, representing a massive mobilisation of the middle classes against the call for the working-class vote.

It is one of the quirks of the story of what happened on 10 April that one of these special constables was none other than Louis Napoleon, soon to become President of the French Republic. His participation in the mobilisation against the Chartists was clearly a statement of intent, to be heard on the streets of France, that he would defend order against 'the mob'.

It was not only in London that tension was reaching a hysterical pitch. Unrest was occurring in the industrial areas of the North, and tension was particularly high in Manchester and Liverpool. At the Chartist Convention, Ernest Jones was calling for simultaneous demonstrations to be organised in all the areas of Chartist influence so that the authorities could not concentrate their forces in London alone. It was clear that the threat from the Chartists was national in scale. Urgent requests went out to magistrates in all the major centres for reports on the situation in their districts. The telegraph companies were temporarily taken over by the government to ensure speedy communications around the country.

The loyalty and morale of the troops were monitored closely. There had been reports of soldiers signing the Charter and even declaring that, if ordered to shoot, they would fire over the heads of the people. Reports of political discussion among soldiers were also cause for some concern. A dozen or so soldiers of the Scottish Fusiliers were heard in conversation in a public house:

> One of them . . . stated that he had an aged father and mother . . . who were reduced in circumstances and who now received for their maintenance from the Parish only three shillings a week – and what use was three shillings a week to an old couple of their age – he, for one, knew others of the same mind, would never fight for any Government or any other system which would behave so to any poor people.[14]

Certainly, Wellington was concerned enough not to billet his troops with civilians in case fraternisation undermined his command.

In London all strategic centres had been fortified. At the Bank of England, the building had been sandbagged and the windows boarded up, leaving only spaces for muskets. Troops were stationed inside, along with the 500 clerks and servants who had been sworn in as special constables and each armed with a brace of pistols, a musket and a cutlass. Other buildings fortified in the same way included East India House, Mansion House, the Guildhall, the Customs House, the Post Office, the Admiralty, the Royal Mint, the

Tower of London and Wellington's home, Apsley House. The government was prepared for revolution.

Whether the Chartists were really prepared for such decisive confrontation is, frankly, more debatable. The force which had been massed so visibly by the state to prevent the procession going ahead elicited different reactions among the Chartists.

There were certainly delegates at the Convention who were of the opinion that, if the authorities were prepared to use violence against them to suppress their just demands, then they must respond in kind. From Edinburgh it was reported that Chartists 'were ready to support their principles at the stake, in the dungeon or on the field'. In the event of the petition being rejected, the Northampton Chartists 'would demand its enactment at the point of a bayonet'.[15] Generally, the delegates from the most economically distressed regions were the most revolutionary in tone.

Among the national leadership, however, vacillation and confusion reigned. Feargus O'Connor had always played to the gallery on the question of moral force and physical force. When addressing the throngs of the 'fustian jackets and unshorn chins' there was no limit to his militancy. In his real leadership of the Chartist movement, however, he was a great deal more ambivalent. Now, in this situation of sharp confrontation between the classes, which allowed no room for artful ambiguities, he began to go to pieces.

As 10 April approached, the pressures on O'Connor began to close, vice-like, upon him. On the one hand, the expectations of the movement were growing in a massive tide which threatened to overwhelm the leadership. On the other hand, the clear intention of the authorities to use violence made a bloodbath not at all unimaginable. O'Connor was convinced, and not without good reason, that an attempt would be made on his life. Indeed, it is a testament to O'Connor's courage and commitment to his movement that he was to have such a visible profile on the day itself.

Despite his personal courage, however, O'Connor began to yield to pressure from the police. The government had wanted to ban the gathering altogether, but this had proved impossible. What they did insist on was that the gathering meet on the other side of the Thames to the Houses of Parliament, and that no mass procession to Parliament take place. Instead only a delegation would be allowed to cross the river to present the petition. O'Connor agreed readily to these conditions.

The Chartist demonstration at Kennington Common, 1848

Finale and debacle

On the morning of 10 April, Chartists gathered at several points in and around London to march to Kennington Common. Stepney Green was a major assembly point, as were Clerkenwell Green and Russell Square. The Stepney band led the procession towards London Bridge. The crowd carried banners with slogans such as 'Liberty, Equality and Fraternity. The Charter and No Surrender' and 'Liberty is Worth Living For and Worth Dying For'. Caps of Liberty were visible here and there, and some wore the colours of the French tricolour. Irish Repealers who joined the procession were cheered as they arrived.

The number who finally arrived at Kennington Common for this monster gathering is not certain. It was probably somewhere between 150,000 and 200,000, although some estimates, particularly from the *Northern Star*, put the figure as high as 500,000.

One thing, however, is certain. O'Connor and the other speakers that day played down any confrontational element in their speeches. No procession would take place to Parliament. Instead a small delegation would present the petition and the demonstrators would disperse peacefully. This in the end was what happened. After the momentous build-up, and the expectations of revolution among both workers and the ruling class, the crisis had quietly passed.

There were those who protested. Cuffay, for example, leapt off the wagon on which he was standing, exclaiming that they were all 'humbugged and betrayed'. But to no avail.

The wealthy were ecstatic with relief. The fear of the lower orders on the part of the upper classes, which had reached such a pitch over the previous weeks and days, now turned into a kind of hysterical contempt.

Firstly, the petition itself was ridiculed. O'Connor had claimed a total of nearly 6 million signatures. After an absurdly short time the clerks appointed to scrutinise the petition declared that only 2 million were genuine – still twice the electorate of the House of Commons. Quite how they arrived at this figure remains a mystery. We can probably assume that the signatures of Lord John Russell, Sir Robert Peel, Queen Victoria, Prince Albert and the Duke of Wellington, which appeared several times each, were forgeries. The petition had also attracted its fair share of obscenities aimed at the government, which the clerks blushingly refused to reveal. After this, however, the real explanation for much of the 'forgery' probably lies with the prejudice of the authorities. Women who had signed, for example, were not included in the 'genuine' count. Where the same hand had signed a number of different names, probably for those who could not write, these too were excluded. Whatever the truth, one thing was clear. The movement was on the defensive and the tide had turned suddenly against the Chartists.

This is not to say that Chartism withered and died after 10 April. On the contrary. The number of Chartist localities actually increased in many parts of the country. Activity also continued. Demonstrations, for example, took place around the trial of John Mitchell, the Irish leader. In May between 50,000 and 60,000 marched through London demanding his release. Indeed, the levels of demonstrations and disturbance, particularly in the northern industrial areas, continued to cause alarm among the propertied classes throughout the summer.

By late summer, however, Chartism no longer represented a serious threat to the established order. Most of the first-rank national leadership, including Ernest Jones and Peter McDouall, had been arrested and jailed. Feargus O'Connor was by now completely taken up with the inquiry into the Land Plan. Many among the second rank of Chartist leaders had also been imprisoned.

The treatment of the Chartists who were imprisoned in 1848 was barbaric. From the point of view of the authorities, these were individuals who had dared to challenge the established order and they were to be made to pay for that insolence. Ernest Jones was imprisoned for two years. It is worth quoting his testimony at length:

> I was kept for more than two years in separate confinement on the silent system, most rigidly enforced – so rigidly that for an involuntary I was sent for three days to a dark cell on bread and water. For the first nineteen months I was kept without books, pen, ink, or paper, and had to sit out that time in a cell, twelve feet by seven, locked up in solitude and silence, without even a table or chair. To this cell (the day cell) were three windows, two without glass but with rough wooden shutters, through which the wind and snow and rain of winter blew all over the place. My night cell was of far smaller dimensions, 9 feet by 4 feet. Its window was unglazed – its shutters did not meet the window frame nor each other by one or two inches. There was an aperture over my bed 18 in. by 12 in., through which the snow and rain fell on me as I slept, saturating my clothes with moisture, so that often the water dripped from them as I put them on. The bed itself was a sack of straw with a piece of carpeting. From this bed I had to go, when I rose at five in the morning, across two yards in my shirt and trousers only, to wash and dress in the open air, after getting wet through in the rain and snow while dressing, and sitting all day in my wet clothes in my fireless cell; for during the first twelve months I was allowed no fire in my day cell. During the intense frost of the winter of '49, I had to break the ice in the stone trough in which I was compelled to wash, in the same water, frequently, that other prisoners had used. The diet was so poor, and often of so revolting a kind, that at last I was unable to walk across my cell without support, through loss of strength. Neither fork nor knife was allowed at meals, and I had to tear my food with my fingers. Bent to the ground with rheumatism, and racked with neuralgia, I applied for permission to have a fire, but this was denied me, as already stated, till the second year of my imprisonment. Then I became so weak that I was compelled to crawl on all fours if I sought to reach the door of my cell to knock for assistance. On one occasion I fell against the grate, and had a narrow escape of being burned to death. It will be remembered that in the year of 1849, the cholera raged so fearfully in London that in one day 417 persons died. During the height of the plague, while suffering from bowel complaint, I was sent to a darkened cell, because I did not

pick the oakum that was brought to me as my daily task ... During all this time, after the first few weeks, I was allowed to hear from my wife and children only once every three months ... [16]

Jones's strength and spirit during these prison years were truly astonishing. He continued to write the poetry for which he became famous. He fashioned an inkwell for himself from soap, and stole writing materials from the governor's office where for a period he was put to work. For paper he used hymn sheets. For ink he even claimed to have used his own blood.

The other Chartists who were sentenced at the same time as Jones all died as a result of the treatment they received. Jones wrote his testimony in response to claims that the Chartists had received lenient treatment after 1848.

With the national leadership behind bars and the rejection of the third and largest petition for the working-class vote, the Chartist movement began to fall into confusion and disarray. Chartism was never really to recover from the anti-climax of 10 April. Apart from brief revivals, for example in 1853, this momentous episode in the history of the British working class was over. The legacy of the Chartists, however, is still very much with us. Many of the arguments which raged within the movement at that time are still relevant today and are reflected in the debates about the significance of the Chartist movement itself.

Song of the Lower Classes
Ernest Jones

We plough and sow – we're so very, very low,
  That we delve in the dirty clay,
Till we bless the plain with the golden grain,
  And the vale with the fragrant hay.
Our place we know – we're so very low,
  'Tis down at the landlord's feet:
We're not too low – the bread to grow
  But too low the bread to eat.

[Chorus]
We're low – we're low – we're very, very low,
  As low as low can be;
The rich are high – for we make them so
  And a miserable lot are we!
  And a miserable lot are we! are we!
  A miserable lot are we!

Down, down we go – we're so very, very low
  To the hell of the deep sunk mines.
But we gather the proudest gems that glow,
  When the crown of a despot shines;
And whenever he lacks – upon our backs
  Fresh loads he deigns to lay,
We're far too low to vote the tax
  But we're not too low to pay.

[Chorus]

We're low, we're low – mere rabble, we know,
  But at our plastic power,
The mould at the lordling's feet will grow
  Into palace and church and tower
Then prostrate fall – in the rich man's hall,
  And cringe at the rich man's door,
We're not too low to build the wall,
  But too low to tread the floor.

[Chorus]

We're low, we're low – we're very, very low,
    Yet from our fingers glide
The silken flow – and the robes that glow,
    Round the limbs of the sons of pride.
And what we get – and what we give,
    We know – and we know our share.
We're not too low the cloth to weave
    But too low the cloth to wear.

[Chorus]

We're low, we're low – we're very, very low,
    And yet when the trumpets ring,
The thrust of a poor man's arm will go
    Through the heart of the proudest king!
We're low, we're low – our place we know,
    We're only the rank and file,
We're not too low – to kill the foe,
    But too low to touch the spoil.

[Chorus]

Chapter 6 Leaders and socialists

Feargus O'Connor

Every generation of struggle throws up its great leaders. Such figures often come to personify the age in which they live and to embody the hopes and ideals of those they lead. In the history of the British working class, however, none can match the flamboyance and stature of Feargus O'Connor.

O'Connor was born of a landed Irish family with radical associations. He was actively involved in the 'Whiteboy' rebellions against British rule in the 1820s. In January 1833 he became the Cork Member of Parliament for the Repeal Party led by Daniel O'Connell.

We get a glimpse of O'Connor's somewhat cavalier style in these early years during the by-election for Dungarvan in the summer of 1834. Dungarvan included the Irish seat of the Duke of Devonshire at Lismore Castle. The borough consistently returned the Duke's own candidate at election time through a combination of patronage and intimidation. On the occasion of the 1834 election, however, O'Connor's intervention turned everything upside down. Mounting the hustings in the town square, he read aloud a letter which he claimed to have been written by the Duke. The letter, read out several times by O'Connor to an incredulous audience, declared the Duke's refusal to direct his tenants how to vote and urged them to support whoever they held to be the best candidate. The estate's tenants flocked to vote for the Repeal candidate. The Duke, of course, had not written the letter in O'Connor's possession, which, upon eventually being challenged, turned out to have carried the signature 'Ebenezer Humbug'.

O'Connor was soon to break with O'Connell over the latter's willingness to compromise with British rule. He was soon also to lose his seat after a technical challenge to his credentials for standing.

He now entered the world of English radicalism and embarked on a political career which was to carry him to a position of near veneration in the hearts and minds of the working class of the late 1830s and 1840s.

O'Connor was a dominating character from every point of view. Physically he was something of a giant, at six foot, in an age when workers suffered stunted growth from arduous labour and poor diet. In personality he projected utter self-confidence, which frequently displayed itself as an overbearing arrogance and a total inability to see error in himself. There was, for example, the episode of O'Connor's fairly inept intervention in the Oldham election of 1835, where he succeeded in splitting radical support, obtaining only 32 votes (he was a completely unknown candidate at this time), and allowing the Tory candidate in. Unabashed he left the town in an open triumphal carriage escorted by his supporters and flying a flag with the inscription 'Roderick O'Connor Monarch of Ireland' – a reminder of his claim to be descended from the kings of Ireland.

At the height of his prominence, O'Connor would travel in procession in open carriages to rapturous applause and adulation. O'Connor's flair for the theatrical was evident on the occasion of his release from prison in 1841. Appearing in a rough, fustian workman's suit he set off in procession from the prison in an open sea-shell shaped carriage of green and pink.

O'Connor brought colour and inspiration to the movement. But he was not the only such personality and he was rivalled for pre-eminence by such figures as the Rev. Joseph Rayner Stephens and Richard Oastler. What decided O'Connor's dominating influence, however, was what proved to be by far his most important contribution to the working-class movement: his paper, the *Northern Star*.

Launched in November 1837, the *Northern Star* rapidly gained a mass working-class readership. By February 1838 it was selling over 10,000 copies a week. By 1839 it had reached a weekly circulation of 50,000, rivalling the daily circulation of *The Times*. Indeed, the Post Office was obliged to hire extra waggons for distribution of the paper around the country.

The *Northern Star* was from the beginning the paper of a movement. The coverage of its pages reflected the extent of its influence as well as the depth of its roots in the working class. Reports came in from all over the country. Correspondents for the *Northern Star* were to be found in almost every town and in the smallest villages. From a purely journalistic point of view it was brilliant, rivalling *The Times* for depth and content, and drawing on the best radical writing talent of the day. The commercial success of the paper meant that profits could be returned to the movement via the financing of agitation: 'every £10 made, was spent in travelling, agitating, donations, subscriptions . . . in support of the cause'.[1]

The popularity of the *Northern Star* was reflected in the subscriptions raised in its support. Five hundred pounds was raised for the launch of the paper from Leeds, Halifax, Bradford, Huddersfield and Hull alone,[2] and money continued to flow in. Indeed, the delivery of the *Northern Star* was something of a weekly event in many localities with people lining the roadsides awaiting its arrival. One handloom weaver from South Lancashire later recalled:

> *The* Northern Star, *the only newspaper that appeared to circulate anywhere, found its way weekly to the Cut side, being subscribed for by my father and five others. Every Sunday morning these subscribers met at our house to hear what prospect there was of the expected 'smash-up' taking place. It was my task to read aloud so that all could hear at the same time; and the comments that were made on the events foreshadowed would have been exceedingly edifying to me were I to hear them now.*[3]

The reading aloud of the *Northern Star*, perhaps by one of the few workers or workers' children able to read, in a coffee room, an inn or a workshop was typical. Such readings could assume some formality or be highly informal. Often a lead article or O'Connor's letter would be read out for collective reflection. This would then be followed by a discussion of the major themes of the address. The following account gives us a flavour of the atmosphere during the tea-break in one Leicester knitters' workshop:

> *Some would seat themselves on the winder's stools, some on bricks, and others, whose frames were at the centre, would sit on their 'seat boards'. Then they would commence a general discussion upon various matters, political, moral and religious. After tea a short article would be read from the* Northern Star, *and this would form the subject matter for consideration and chat during the remainder of the day.*[4]

One working-class radical has left us with this sketch of another such regular reading:

> *Another early recollection is that of a Sunday morning gathering in a humble kitchen. The most constant of our visitors was a crippled shoemaker . . . Larry . . . made his appearance every Sunday morning, as regular as clockwork, with a copy of the* Northern Star, *damp from the press, for the purpose of hearing some member of our household read out to him and others 'Feargus's letter'. The paper had first to be dried before the fire, and then carefully and evenly cut, so as not to damage a single line*

of the almost sacred production. This done, Larry, placidly smoking his cutty pipe, which he occasionally thrust into the grate for a light, settled himself to listen with all the rapture of a devotee in a tabernacle to the message of the great Feargus, watching and now and then turning the little joint as it hung and twirled before the kitchen fire, and interjecting occasional chuckles of approval as some particularly emphatic sentiment was read aloud.[5]

The public reading of the *Northern Star* gave it a far larger audience than that indicated by its recorded sales. Copies would be passed with great care, and some solemnity, from one reader to the next. Alternatively, a local agent might lend the paper out for specified periods. By April 1839 the *Northern Star* could claim a readership of 400,000.

The mass readership of the *Northern Star*, together with the openness of its pages to debate and criticism, meant that it rose above being simply a newspaper. It became a crucial element in fertilising the growing working-class consciousness of the time. It gave the Chartist movement a sense of its own magnitude. A report from the smallest meeting in the most remote village seemed significant in the pages of the *Northern Star*. It brought great events closer to workers and it made their leaders, not only O'Connor, familiar figures.

O'Connor, in his final years, was a tragic figure. The fiasco of 1848 and his waning influence in the movement after his release from prison in 1850 conspired to affect his mind. He became incoherent in public as well as in private, and was often seen muttering aloud to himself as he descended into drink and morbidity. But in the *Northern Star* he had begun a tradition of the working-class paper as communicator and organiser for which, above all else, he should be remembered.

The Charter around which the Chartist movement revolved was explicitly a manifesto of political reform. The 'six points' did not address the economic grievances of the working class of the day. The general view was that once the working-class vote was achieved, the political power this would bring would be enough in itself to improve the daily life of the worker. This separation of the political from the economic, however, did not reflect the realities of the Chartist movement. The energy which was the driving force of the movement bubbled up from deep wells of resentment at the material conditions which workers faced. Certainly the Victorian ruling class, too, paid no heed to such a separation. While the governments of the day used political repression and violence against the Chartists, the large employers responded to the movement with lockouts and attacks on trade union organisation – they fought on every front simultaneously.

The logic and momentum of a movement for reform which at the same time, almost in spite of itself, struck so heavily at the foundations of capitalism began to generate new ideas that went beyond this contradiction. It was this conflict within Chartism that produced the first significant socialist leaders of the British working-class movement. It was not that there had not been socialist ideas present before this. But what was different now was the scale of audience they addressed. Three names stand out from the period: James Bronterre O'Brien; Ernest Jones; and George Julian Harney. These were all figures of national stature who, at different points in the Chartist period, exercised dominant influence within the movement.

James Bronterre O'Brien

Bronterre O'Brien was the nearest Chartism had to a theorist of the movement. Later dubbed the 'Chartist Schoolmaster', he entered the world of working-class political life as a young radical lawyer, influenced by the ideas both of the Owenites and of the French Revolution. He was especially struck by the figure of Robespierre, whose memory he defended throughout his life. His intellectual outlook, however, had been shaped by the radical communism of Francis Noel Babeuf.

Babeuf had occupied an extreme left position during the French Revolution. He advocated the abolition of property and conspired for the restitution of the democratic constitution of 1793 in which the chamber of electors had been decided by popular suffrage. The 'Conspiracy of Equals' was eventually suppressed by the new French republic and Babeuf himself was executed.

To O'Brien, Babeuf represented the highest idealism of the French Revolution and he determined to bring his message of radical egalitarianism to a British working-class audience. This he did in his translation of a work by one of Babeuf's close collaborators, Buonarroti. Buonarroti's *History of Babeuf's Conspiracy for Equality* was published in 1836 with O'Brien's comments. In justification of the translation, O'Brien enthused:

> *Babeuf's 'Conspiracy for Equality' appears to me the only event of the kind recorded in history that was sincerely and comprehensively designed for the benefit of human kind . . . a plot for the emancipation of France – for the regeneration and*

happiness of mankind. It was a conspiracy to restore the democratic Constitution of 1793, and . . . the reign of political and social equality.[6]

O'Brien's socialism, spelt out in his ten-page pamphlet *State Socialism*, around which he hoped the movement would unite, was still of an essentially reformist nature. It was not a vision in which workers would directly control society. Rather society would be organised for the working class through the state. Nonetheless, this argument for the nationalisation of industry and of the land, together with O'Brien's belief in the potential of automation to lighten labour's load, has a peculiarly modern ring to it.

O'Brien was later to move rightwards and into the camp of the moral force Chartists. In the early intellectual flux of the British working-class movement, however, O'Brien's ideas represent an important milestone in popularising the socialist argument to a mass audience.

Ernest Jones

Ernest Jones was a comparative latecomer to the Chartist movement. He had been born of a wealthy family and trained as a barrister. His conversion to the cause of Chartism was total and his life was to become an example of the kind of utter dedication and self-sacrifice which only great movements in history can inspire.

Jones's first contact with Chartism came via his joining of the Fraternal Democrats. This brought him into contact and correspondence with Marx and Engels, who were to become the principal influence for most of his political career. His ability as an orator carried him quickly to prominence and he soon became deputy-editor of the *Northern Star*.

Jones had been moving towards socialism at the time of his arrest following the 1848 gathering. By the time of his release in early 1850 he was firmly in the socialist camp. He was soon speaking and writing to this effect and was one of the first to begin arguing for the need to build a working-class socialist party.

The atmosphere within the Chartist movement had also shifted distinctly to the left. The repression following 1848 had once again forced new directions on the movement. As one article in the *Red Republican* put it:

Chartism in 1850 is a different thing from Chartism in 1840. The leaders of the English Proletarians have proved that they are true Democrats, and no shams, by going ahead so rapidly in the last

Ernest Jones: Chartist and socialist

few years. They have Progressed from the idea of a simple political reform to the idea of a Social Revolution.[7]

Jones was now to enter into closer collaboration with Marx and Engels. In July 1850 he joined the staff of the Red Republican. Shortly afterwards he launched his own paper, *Notes to the People*, the editorship of which he briefly shared with Marx. In the ferment of ideas on the left wing of Chartism, the ideas of Marx, as propounded in the *Communist Manifesto* – first published in English in the autumn of 1850 – were becoming increasingly influential. It was these ideas which Jones began to expound to enthusiastic meetings. What was distinctive about Jones was his insistence not only that economic concerns must be linked to political struggle – the 'Big Loaf', he said, must be held alongside the 'Cap of Liberty' – but also that 'the Poor alone can win the battle of the Poor'.

> *Therefore, the capitalists of all kinds will be our foes as long as they exist, and carry on against us a war to the very knife. Therefore they must Be Put Down. Therefore we Must have class against class – that is, all the oppressed on the one side, and all the oppressors on the other. An amalgamation of classes is impossible where an amalgamation of interests is impossible also . . . CLASS AGAINST CLASS – all other mode of proceeding is mere moonshine.[8]*

Jones's partnership with Marx and Engels, however, was not all plain sailing. They despaired, for example, at his open hostility to the trade unions of the day, which were not as revolutionary as Jones wished them to be. They were similarly critical of his tendency to condemn strikes as attempts merely to ameliorate the conditions which capitalism inflicted upon the working class. Indeed, this friction was to result in a final rift in their relationship towards the end of Jones's life.

Nonetheless Jones stands out as one of the great socialists of the early movement. He was key, for example, in setting up the International Committee which served as a historical link between the internationalism of the Fraternal Democrats in the 1840s and the First International of Marx and Engels in the 1860s. In all of this Jones, along with Harney, was one of the first really significant exponents of Marxism in the British working-class movement.

George Julian Harney

If O'Brien had identified himself with Robespierre, George Julian Harney tended to see himself as the Marat of the movement. Marat had stood on the radical left of the French Revolution and now Harney stood clearly on the socialist left of Chartism. Harney, too, was influenced by the communism of Babeuf.

Harney's first contact with Engels came with their meeting in the autumn of 1843. Harney was the older and more politically mature – Engels still being influenced by the philosophical radicalism of the German intellectual circles. Harney, for example, routinely spoke at Chartist meetings of the irreconcilable conflict of interests between the classes. To Engels this was a revelation, and the working-class world in which Harney moved was an education to him. It was at this time that Engels began to shift away from the old obsessions with philosophy to a real concern with the class struggle working in society and also towards a study of political economy.

In 1845 Engels had brought Marx to Britain to witness the British workers' movement first hand and to study the British economists. With Harney they established the Communist Corresponding Society to link together radicals all over the continent. By this time the ideas of Marx and Engels, regarding the class nature of society and the class struggle as the key to understanding history, were the focus around which a number of radical groups were coalescing. The result, in June 1847, was the formation of the Communist League. In all of this Harney was by far the most important English participant. Indeed, his ideas and statements at this time anticipated those of Marx and Engels:

> It is in the interests of land-lords and money-lords to keep the nations divided: but it is the interests of the proletarians, everywhere oppressed by the same sort of task masters and

everywhere defrauded of the fruits of their industry by the same description of plunderers, it is their interest to unite. And they will unite. From the loom, the anvil, and the plow, from the hut, the garret, and the cellar, will come forth, and are even now coming forth, the apostles of fraternity and destined saviours of humanity.[9]

Harney, however, was no theorist. He was, above all, an activist and an organiser. After 1848 he enthusiastically backed Ernest Jones's plans to extend the political base of Chartism. In 1849 the Fraternal Democrats, in which Harney had been so central as a founding member, and which had been suppressed under the Alien Act, began to enjoy something of a resurgence. Harney now himself re-emerged as a popular leader.

Harney's newfound prominence was not an isolated phenomenon. The entire Chartist movement, still commanding a massive working-class audience, was surging to the left under the impact of the continental revolutions, the failure of the Kennington Common gathering and the collapse of the old leadership. After a sharp break with O'Connor, Harney and the Fraternal Democrats took executive control of the NCA. Chartism was now officially a socialist movement and the shift was marked by the launch of Harney's new paper – the *Red Republican* – which, in the 9 November 1850 edition, carried the first serialised publication of the *Communist Manifesto*. In the first edition Harney spelt out the position of the paper:

Will they charge us with being 'enemies to order'? We shall prove that their order is an 'organised hypocrisy'. Will they charge us with contemplating spoliation? We shall prove that they themselves are spoliators and robbers. Will they accuse us of being 'bloodthirsty democrats'? We shall prove our accusers to be remorseless traffickers in the lives of their fellow creatures . . .[10]

This move to the left was strongly reflected in the Chartist Convention of 1851. The programme agreed at the Convention was a distinctly social democratic one, calling for social as well as political reform. As *The Times* put it, it combined industrial democracy with industrial socialism.

The Convention of 1851 represents a high point of socialist influence within Chartism and also of Harney's leadership. This high point, however, came as Chartism was on the wane as an organised movement. The trade cycle was entering an upswing and workers were finding that, if they used their trade union muscle, they could extract concessions from their employers. The argument for a complete rejection of capitalism and its replacement with a socialist society, therefore, had less resonance than previously. Nonetheless, against those voices today who complain that politics are an alien intrusion into the normal workings of trade union affairs, we should remind ourselves that, on the contrary, politics, and specifically socialist politics, are natural to our movement, and were present at the start.

Chapter 7　Marxism and the Chartist movement

Marx, Engels and the Chartists

Chartism, as an organised movement, did not officially end its existence until 1860. However, after the repression of 1848 its energy as a national focus for working-class rebellion was spent. Ever since, Chartism's detractors have berated its memory with the charge that it failed in its aims. After all, the governments of the day did not give the working class the vote or increased political rights. These things came much later. But such a view utterly misses the significance of Chartism as the first mass working-class movement in history. Moreover, it completely fails to appreciate the extent to which the Chartists did unalterably change the climate of opinion in British society – both in the ruling circles of the country and among workers themselves – as to the potential threat the industrial working class represented to the established order.

The story of the Chartists does not, in fact, finish with the winding up of the NCA. Individual Chartists went on to play a vital role in working-class radical politics as councillors and publishers, in agitation for reform and in the organisation of the early trade unions.

Reunions also took place to reminisce or to mark significant events. The last of these was probably the gathering at Halifax to celebrate the passing of the third Reform Act in 1885. These occasions could often rekindle the old controversies. When the Dundee veterans met together in 1873, a fierce argument broke out over the choice of meeting place – a temperance hall!

The fortunes of the old comrades were as varied as the movement had itself been. While a number prospered in different ways, most did not fare so well. The leaders of the Newport uprising, for example, with the exception of John Frost, remained exiled and in chains on the penal colonies of Van Diemen's Island and Port Arthur. Many ended their lives in extreme poverty. The last recorded sighting of the Chartist leader John Arnott was when he was seen begging in the Strand in 1865. On a lecture tour in West Yorkshire,

Harney was forced to send for a tailor to mend his only pair of trousers while he had to remain in bed till the job was done. The organisers of one meeting found that they had to buy a new shirt and front for the old Chartist Samuel Kydd, before he could speak.

The influence of individual Chartists is particularly impressive in the early labour movement in the United States. Many prominent national and local Chartists had emigrated to the New World to escape Queen Victoria's jails. As they were unable to shed their convictions in their new life, their names came to pepper the history of the American trade union and radical movements. The names of a few will suffice to illustrate the point: the Yorkshire miner John Bates was founder of a mining union in Pennsylvania; John Siney of Wigan became the first president of the Miners' National Association; the Staffordshire miner Thomas Lloyd was president of the American Miners' Association; the Lancashire weaver Richard Hinton organised workers in Lawrence, Massachusetts; the Southampton carpenter Richard Trevellick became a leader of the National Labor Union; the Sheffield shoemaker Thomas Phillips became president of the Boot and Shoe Workers' Union; Andrew Cameron published the *Workingman's Advocate* and played a leading role in the Typographical Union. Indeed, the children of the Chartists also went on to play their role. Thomas Morgan, son of a Birmingham Chartist nail-maker, was the first president of the Brassworkers' Union and Samuel Fielden, son of the Todmorden Chartist, was a prominent figure in the American trade union movement.[1]

These names give only a glimpse of the contribution Chartists made to the working-class movements of the countries to which they emigrated or were exiled. The impact of Chartism on our history, however, goes far beyond the lives of such individuals.

Chartism lives with us today in the continuing relevance of the ideas of Marx and Engels. The influence of Chartism on Marx and Engels has nowhere near been as widely recognised as it should have been. It is true that there is no single substantial piece of writing on the Chartists to be found in their collected works. What we do see, however, are constant references and sidelines. Time and again Marx and Engels draw on and generalise from the Chartist experience to the extent that it comes to permeate nearly all of their work.

It should first of all be understood that both Marx and Engels were actively involved in the Chartist movement. They were on personal terms with nearly all of its leading figures. They wrote regularly for the Chartist press and, as we have seen, by the late

1840s their ideas were becoming increasingly influential. This was shown clearly when the Chartist 'Labour Parliament', called against the background of a massive strike wave in March of 1853, invited Marx to attend as an honorary delegate. In 1855 we find a colourful passage in which Marx describes a massive Chartist demonstration against a bill banning Sunday trading, which he attended in Hyde Park – an occasion, incidentally, on which Marx narrowly escaped arrest.

In fact many of the continental *émigrés* involved themselves in one way or another with the Chartists. Much more important is the way in which the Chartist movement, against the backdrop of early industrial capitalism and Britain's world political and economic pre-eminence, profoundly shaped Marx's and Engels' thinking.

In the nineteenth century, Britain was the foremost industrial country in Europe, and in many ways the economic powerhouse of the world. The revolution which had paved the way for the explosive expansion of industry in Britain had occurred more than a century before the revolution of 1789 in France – Britain's nearest rival.

The highly industrialised nature of British society had produced sharp polarisation along lines of class. As Engels put it:

> *Only in England has industry attained such dimensions that it is the focal point of the whole national interest, of all the conditions of existence for every class. But industry consists on the one hand of the industrial bourgeoisie and on the other of the industrial proletariat, and all the other elements comprising the nation are increasingly grouped around these opposed classes. Here therefore, where the only point that matters is who shall rule, the industrial capitalists or the industrial workers, here, if anywhere, is the ground where the class struggle in its modern form can be decided and where the industrial proletariat on the one hand has the strength to win political power and on the other hand finds the material means, the productive forces which enable it to make a total social revolution and ultimately to eliminate class contradictions.*[2]

It was such social conditions, then, which made it possible for Marx and Engels to focus clearly on the class contradictions that ran through society. Such conditions were nowhere near so developed in other European countries. The concept of class, however, was not only of use in analysing the contemporary political scene. It was to become something altogether more important. In Marx's hands it was to become the key by which history itself could be opened and understood – and by which it could be changed.

The early socialists

Socialists before Marx had railed against the horrors of capitalism. They had dreamed of change. They had constructed utopias in their imaginations which could be marvellously progressive for their day at the same time as being somewhat quixotic – especially to the modern reader. There were those such as Claude Henri Saint-Simon who yearned for a rationally ordered society where human happiness could be administrated through a kind of scientific calculus. Such a society would be governed by the *savants* – the industrialists and scientists of the day. Despite the undemocratic nature of Saint-Simon's vision – workers, for example, were to be denied the vote – as well as the rather robotic notion of human happiness, there were progressive aspects to what he was attempting to do. Saint-Simon rejected the anarchy of the marketplace, for example, and replaced it with the idea of a planned society. He yearned for the clearing away of feudal ideology and superstition and for a world based on science, culture and learning.

Another great name among the utopian socialists was Charles Fourier. Fourier was appalled at the miseries and moral corruption which capitalism produced. The world of commerce, for example, he referred to as 'probing the stink of moral filth which is called the bordel of exchange and brokerage'. He placed the liberation of women at the centre of his world-view of social change. He talked of the alienation caused by capitalist industrial society and a utopia of human fulfilment. Of all the utopian socialists, Fourier was probably also the one most given to bizarre flights of fancy. He spelled out the details of his new world in precise detail. People were to live in 'phalanxes' of 1,600 individuals. Work would be organised in a highly regimented way. He used the idea of sorting peas to explain this – young children would remove the peas from the pod, older ones would grade them and so on. For every animal there would be an 'anti-animal', 'the anti-lion', the 'anti-leopard', etc. There were even to be seas of lemonade!

Apart from the straightforwardly comical sides to some of the ideas of the utopian socialists, what united most of them, including those such as Etienne Cabet in France and Robert Owen in England, was the notion that class interests between workers and capitalists could be harmonised within a rational society. None really saw the abolition of rich and poor as being essential. Most crucially, without a concept of class informing their systems, and being central to the transition from capitalism to socialism, they could see no way of achieving change which could grow out of existing realities. In the end their utopias were based on a moral objection to capitalism and were merely counter-posed to it with so many statements as to what might be possible. Fourier vaguely hoped that some wealthy benefactor might finance the whole experiment. True to his convictions, in the latter years of his life, he placed advertisements and would return each lunchtime to his front door in the hope of meeting such a benefactor – who, of course, never came.

The importance of the working class

In the social conditions we have described, against the background of the Chartist movement and with the ideas of Marx and Engels crystallising around the concept of an irreconcilable conflict of class interests, a very different notion of social change began to emerge. Engels in his work *Socialism: Utopian and Scientific* explained the impact that the class struggles of the time had on his and Marx's thinking:

> In 1831, the first working class rising took place in Lyons; between 1838 and 1842, the first national working class movement, that of the English Chartists, reached its height. The class struggle between the proletariat and the bourgeoisie came to the front in the history of the most advanced countries in Europe, in proportion to the development, upon the one hand, of modern industry, upon the other, of the newly acquired political supremacy of the bourgeoisie. Facts more and more strenuously gave the lie to the teachings of bourgeois economy as to the identity of the interests of capital and labour, as to the universal harmony and universal prosperity that would be the consequence of unbridled competition. All these things could no longer be ignored, any more than the French and English Socialism, which was their theoretical, though very imperfect, expression . . .
>
> The new facts made imperative a new examination of all past history. Then it was seen that all past history, with the exception of its primitive stages, was the history of class struggles . . .
>
> From that time forward Socialism was no longer an accidental discovery of this or that ingenious brain, but the necessary outcome of the struggle between two historically developed classes – the proletariat and the bourgeoisie.[3]

The enormity of this leap in thinking cannot be overstated. Capitalism was now seen in its historical location as one economic mode of society among many which had existed before – tribal societies, slave society, serf society, feudal society, and so on. Marx and Engels then, in their new 'historical materialist' perspective on human society, were developing an objection to capitalism which was no longer based upon a merely moral revulsion to its horrors – which, of course, they felt. Their objection to capitalism was now that it had outlived its progressive role in history. It had certainly increased the forces of production in society on a massive scale. But more than this it contained within itself the potential of its own dissolution. This potential lay in the new social force that it had created – the working class – which could be seen in its greatest numbers and highest level of organisation and consciousness in Britain.

In Britain also, Marx and Engels saw a working class that was not only politically advanced, but which stood head and shoulders above the middle classes of the time in cultural terms:

> ... Chartism has its strength in the working men, the proletarians. Socialism does not form a closed political party, but on the whole it derives its supporters from the lower middle classes and the proletarians. Thus, in England, the remarkable fact is seen that the lower the position of a class in society, the more 'uneducated' it is in the usual sense of the word, the more closely is it connected with progress, and the greater its future ... In England, for three hundred years the educated and all the learned people have been deaf and blind to the signs of the times. Well known throughout the world is the pitiful routine of the English universities, compared with which our German colleges are like gold ... Everywhere there is inconsistency and hypocrisy, while the striking economic tracts of the Socialists and partly also of the Chartists are thrown aside with contempt and find readers only among the lower classes. Strauss' Das Leben Jesu was translated into English. Not a single 'respectable' book publisher wanted to print it; finally it appeared in separate parts, 3d. per part, and that was done by the publishing house of a minor but energetic antiquarian. The same thing occurred with the translations of Rousseau, Voltaire, Holbach, etc. Byron and Shelley are read almost exclusively by the lower classes; no 'respectable' person could have the works of the latter on his desk without coming into the most terrible disrepute.[4]

This is not to suggest that either Marx or Engels had a rosy view of the working class. As we have seen, there was not only an advanced and progressive aspect to the nineteenth-century working class, along with a strong class consciousness, but also a whole range of tendencies which led away from a socialist consciousness and which were sometimes frankly reactionary.

What put Marx and Engels leagues ahead of their contemporaries on the European radical scene was their understanding of the contradictory nature of class consciousness under capitalism. Most were involved either in small sects or in conspiratorial groups of one sort or another. Such 'revolutionists' saw only the reactionary side of the workers' movements of their day. They did not see the whole picture. Rather than attempt to relate in an open fashion to the working class, they preferred to live in the self-selected world of pure, untainted, revolutionary organisation:

> The sects formed by these initiators are abstentionists by their very nature, i.e. alien to all real action, – politics, strikes, coalitions, or, in a word, to any united movement. The mass of the proletariat always remains indifferent or even hostile to their propaganda. The Paris and Lyons workers did not want the Saint-Simonians, the Fourierists, the Icarians, any more than the Chartists and the English trade unionists wanted the Owenists.[5]

Because of their observations of and involvement in the Chartist movement, Marx and Engels fast came to the understanding that it was possible to be totally involved in the struggles of the working class at the same time as waging a battle of ideas within the working class for socialism. Engels expressed this well in a letter to Marx regarding their ally in the movement, Ernest Jones:

> Jones is moving in quite the right direction and we may well say that, without our doctrine, he would never have discovered how, on the one hand, one can not only maintain the only possible basis for the reconstruction of the Chartist party ... the instinctive class hatred of the workers for the industrial bourgeoisie – but also enlarge and develop it, so laying the foundations for enlightening propaganda and how, on the other, one can still be progressive and resist the workers' reactionary appetites and their prejudices.[6]

One way in which the British working class stood out from the working classes of the other European nations was its strong sense of political independence. In the rest of Europe, although strong and frequently revolutionary working classes existed, under the tyrannical monarchies of the *ancien régime* workers still tended to follow behind the radical middle class. In Britain, workers generally stood apart from the middle class and the leadership of the Chartist movement was explicit in its rejection of any notion of alliances between the working class and other social groups. There were aberrations here and there, particularly during times of retreat. Some leaders did come to associate themselves with middle-class radicalism during the difficult years of the 1840s. But what typified the workers' movement in Britain was self-reliance.

This belief in self-emancipation within the working class in Britain was to leave a deep impression on Marx and Engels and was to develop as a resonant theme throughout their works. 'The emancipation of the working classes', as Marx put it, 'must be conquered by the working classes themselves.'

The political independence that characterised most of the Chartist movement was in part due simply to the size of the working class compared to other classes in Britain. Certainly, the proportion of workers within society, and the scale of urbanisation, were far greater than that of any other European nation. In France perhaps one-third of the working population lived in the cities, two-thirds in the rural areas. In Britain these figures were reversed – two-thirds of the population were urbanised.

The huge size of the working class relative to other groups in society, in Marx's view, gave the demand for universal suffrage a significance it did not have on the Continent. In France the demand for universal suffrage was the demand of the left wing of the middle classes. In a situation where the bulk of the population lived in the politically backward country regions, this demand did not represent any great threat to the existing system. In Britain, however, where the working class was so much bigger than the rural population and where it had already demonstrated its readiness to take dramatic action to achieve its aims, the working-class vote was a much more threatening prospect to the establishment.

From the late 1860s and early 1870s, the beginning of the era of Victorian reform, a whole social machinery was built around the need of the establishment to limit the horizons of a newly enfranchised working class. These were the years in which newly emergent trade unions hitched themselves to the Liberal Party which had been refashioned from the Whigs. Legislation was introduced which led to factory and public health reform. Public education was expanded. All of this had the effect of incorporating working-class politics into the mainstream in a way that could be controlled by the ruling class of the day.

In the 1840s, however, no such infrastructure had been built. In these circumstances the demand for the working-class vote had the potential to become a more fundamental threat to capitalism itself, as workers were forced to fight against a hostile system to attain political equality. In England, then, a political demand for the vote could grow over into a fight for social emancipation. If, to the modern reader, Marx appears to overstate the extent to which the working-class vote would put power into the hands of the working class, it is because he could see clearly this revolutionary potential:

> *The six points of the Charter... contain nothing but the demand of Universal Suffrage, and of the conditions without which Universal Suffrage would be illusory for the working class... But Universal Suffrage is the equivalent of political power for the working class of England, where the proletariat forms the large majority of the population, where, in a long, though underground civil war, it has gained a clear consciousness of its position as a class, and where even the rural districts know no longer any peasants, but only landlords, industrial capitalists (farmers) and hired labourers. The carrying of Universal Suffrage in England would, therefore, be a far more socialistic measure than anything which has been honoured with that name on the Continent.*[7]

And later, in a different piece, he wrote:

> *Universal Suffrage, which was regarded as the motto of universal brotherhood in the France of 1848, has become a battle cry in England. There universal suffrage was the direct content of the revolution, here, revolution is the direct content of universal suffrage.*[8]

In understanding the significance of the demand for political equality within capitalism, Marx and Engels were again streets ahead of their contemporaries. The fashion in radical circles of the time was to dismiss such demands as either conservative or irrelevant – a diversion from the real task of total emancipation. Influenced by the Chartist movement, Marx and Engels had come to understand that under bourgeois rule workers would tend to articulate their demands in the language of the bourgeoisie. In an angry rebuttal to a contemporary, Marx and Engels wrote:

> *He... imagines that citizenship is a matter of indifference to the proletarians, after he has first assumed that they have it... The workers attach so much importance to citizenship, i.e., to active citizenship, that where they have it, for instance in America, they 'make good use' of it, and where they do not have it, they strive to obtain it.*[9]

However, this concern within the Chartist movement for political emancipation, and its lack of a conscious grasp of the social roots of both the condition of the working class and of Chartism itself, was ultimately its downfall:

> . . . the misfortune of the workers in the summer insurrection of 1842 was precisely that they did not know whom to fight against. The evil they suffered was social – and social evils cannot be abolished as the monarchy or privileges are abolished. Social evils cannot be cured by the People's Charter, and the people sensed this . . . Social evils need to be studied and understood, and this the mass of the workers has not yet done up till now. The great achievement of the uprising was that England's most vital question, the question of the final destiny of the working class, was, as Carlyle says, raised in a manner audible to every thinking ear in England. The question can no longer be evaded. England must answer it or perish.[10]

The centrality of revolution

So the question had been posed. But the answer was still unclear. Most workers still thought in terms of a 'legal revolution'. When confronted, even by only handfuls of dragoons, with the illegality of their actions, workers became uncertain and irresolute. Their anger did not allow them to fall back; but without a clear identification of capitalism, rather than a government, as the enemy, neither could they see a way forward if the government would not budge. The result in 1842 was that workers remained doggedly on strike until savings ran out and empty stomachs drove them back to work. The Chartists sought a political answer to a social condition. At certain crucial moments, most notably in 1842 and 1848, their inability to resolve this contradiction in real life led to confusion, vacillation and, ultimately, failure.

There is one more sense in which the Chartist experience profoundly shaped the thinking of Marx and Engels. This was in their internationalism. Ruling the most industrialised country in the world also meant that the British ruling class was by far the most powerful ruling class in the world. This also meant, of course, that Britain was the dominant colonial power. Any movement for national liberation that challenged the colonial carve-up of the world, even if against an oppressor other than Britain, would have Britain to contend with. The struggle for national liberation, then, could only finally succeed with the defeat of the British ruling class by its own working class. As Marx wrote in 1848:

A revolution of the economic relations in any country of the European continent, in the whole European continent without England, is a storm in a tea cup. Industrial and commercial relations within each nation are governed by its intercourse with other nations, and depend on its relations with the world market. But the world market is dominated by England, and England is dominated by the bourgeoisie.[11]

At a speech to celebrate the seventeenth anniversary of the Polish uprising of 1830, Marx drew out the political conclusions:

The victory of the English proletarians over the English bourgeoisie is, therefore, decisive for the victory of all the oppressed over their oppressors. Hence Poland must be liberated not in Poland but in England. So you Chartists must not simply express pious wishes for the liberation of nations. Defeat your own internal enemies and you will then be able to pride yourselves on having defeated the entire old society.[12]

We can see then that in a fundamental sense the Chartist movement formed a backdrop to the course of Marx's and Engels' intellectual and political development. More than this, it posed and answered questions which were to be of enduring importance for future generations of workers. It gave Marx and Engels a way past the utopias of the early socialists as well as the conspiracies of the radical sects. It demonstrated to them how demands for reforms within the system could grow over into a challenge to the system itself. It showed how the struggles of one national working class could link with those of another. As a living, breathing, active movement it showed them that a new historical class, complex as it was, could become conscious of itself and of its power to change the world.

Too often the Chartists have been assessed solely on the question of the vote. In fact the Chartists wanted much more than this. What they fought for was ill defined and even, at times, contradictory. But to the extent that they had a vision, it was always of a different kind of society, one in which workers controlled their own lives without a constant sense of anxiety about how they might feed themselves and their children or survive the next economic slump. Many Chartists spoke of the Charter as being a 'knife and fork' question and of 'the Charter and something more'.

The Chartists had chosen the platform of electoral reform, but not because they dreamed of a future in which everybody would enjoy the privilege of putting a cross on a piece of paper once every five years for a government which did not listen to them. The movement had itself grown out of many disparate strands of struggle which fused together around a political demand. Both the sources which had flowed into the river of Chartism and the vision which inspired it were complex and multifaceted. They did not just want the vote for its own sake. They laid down their lives for the Charter because they thought it would change society.

Schoolbook histories of the Chartists, and indeed even some much respected academic tomes, finish their accounts with the platitude that everything that the Charter demanded has come to pass. Aside from being simply inaccurate – annual parliaments, for example, are hardly the norm in British politics – the implication is that in the end it was gradualism that won the day, and not revolutionary struggle. In this view of history, democracy, such as we have it, has flowed seamlessly from capitalism itself. But the granting of the vote to workers came eventually only after decades of struggle and sacrifice.

Bourgeois democracy, the working-class vote, the political rights we are forced constantly to defend, grew, not from capitalism, but rather from the contradictions of capitalism. As capitalism developed throughout the course of the nineteenth century, it destroyed the old rural backwardness and spawned a class which in size, cohesion and intelligence had the power and the interest to destroy capitalism and the misery it inflicted. This class, the working class, developed its awareness of this power as workers were forced again and again to resist a system which was dependent upon them for their labour, and which simultaneously destroyed and alienated their lives.

For the capitalists of the day, the choice was between reform and repression. They repeatedly demonstrated that they were quite prepared to spill blood should they see fit. But a safer path by far proved to be accommodation and concession on the terrain of political rights – so long as this did not interfere with economic exploitation. In the end, against all their instincts, they were forced to concede reform.

The tactical calculations of the capitalist class in grappling with a new, difficult and dangerous working class, however, were only one side of the process. Something else, much more important, was happening. As workers struggled against political repression, they were becoming class-conscious. The language of nineteenth-century liberalism, the concepts of freedom, equality, citizenship, justice, rights and so on, which had been generated by the great European bourgeois revolutions, were becoming meaningful to workers only as they struggled collectively against the very system which had produced them. As workers combined against low wages and exploitation, they learned that such concepts could be turned against their oppressors in a new language – the language of a struggle, not simply of the poor of a certain region, or of the workers of a particular trade, but of an entire class for a better world. From 1838 to 1848 the Charter was the lens which brought this new working-class consciousness into brilliant focus.

The Chartists were the inspiration of a generation of workers, as they are an inspiration to us today. They fought, suffered and even died that we might walk taller and enjoy the rights of expression and organisation against the same system which they fought against. To the Chartists, with all their faults, goes the unique honour that they were the first. The opening chapter of the British working-class movement culminates in Chartism – a mass movement with a national profile and an internationalist outlook. Their struggle goes on and socialists today carry their banner. We must learn from their mistakes and complete the task they set for themselves – to found society anew.

The New World (extract)
Ernest Jones, written in his prison cell

In sunny clime behold an empire rise,
Fair is its ocean, glorious as its skies!
'Mid seas serene of mild pacific smiles –
Republic vast of federated isles
Sleepy Tradition, lingering, loves to rest,
Confiding Child! on calm Tahiti's breast.
But Science gathers, with gigantic arms,
In one embrace, the South's diffusive charms
Nor there alone she rears the bright domain
Throughout the world expands her hallowing reign.
Then, bold aspiring as immortal thought,
Launched in the boundless, mounts the aeronaut;
While o'er the earth they drive the cloudy team,
Electric messenger and car of steam;
And guide and govern on innocuous course,
The explosive mineral's propelling force;
Or, mocking distance, send on rays of light,
Love's homeborn smiles to cheer the wanderer's sight,
Mechanic power then ministers to health,
And lengthening leisure gladdens greatening wealth;
Brave alchemy, the baffled hope of old,
Then forms the diamond and concretes the gold;
No fevered lands with burning plagues expire,
But draw the rain as Franklin drew the fire;
Or far to mountains guide the floating hail,
And whirl on barren rocks its harmless flail,
Then the weird magnet, bowed by mightier spell,
Robbed of its secret, yields its power as well;
With steely fingers on twin dials placed,
The thoughts of furthest friends are instant traced;
And those fine sympathies that, like a flame,
Fibre to fibre, and frame to frame,
That superstition, in its glamour-pride,
At once misunderstood, and misapplied,
As virtue ripens, shall be all revealed,
When man deserves the trust – such arms to wield
Then shall be known, what fairy love mistaught,
When fancy troubled Truth's instinctive thought,
Then he who filled with life each rolling wave,
And denizens to every dewdrop gave,

Left not this hollow globe's in caverned place.
Then shall the eye, with wide extended sight,
Translate the starry gospel of the night;
And not as now, when narrower bounds are set,
See, but not read, the shining alphabet.
Unhooded knowledge then shall freely scan
That mighty world of breathing wonders – man!
How act and will are one, shall stand defined;
How heart is feeling, and how brain is mind.
Then each disease shall quit the lightened breast;
By pain tormented while by vice oppressed;
And Life's faint step to Death's cool threshold seem
The gentle passing of a pleasant dream.

Table of events

1830
Whig government formed. Wide expectations of political reform.

1832
Reform Bill passed against background of agitation.

1834

January   Launch of the Grand National Consolidated Trades Union, which rapidly becomes a mass membership organisation.
March   Tolpuddle Martyrs sentenced.
July   Passing of the Poor Law Amendment Act.
August   Dissolution of the Grand National Consolidated Trades Union.

1835
Working Men's Associations and Radical Associations formed in Scotland and the North.
September   O'Connor on tour.

1836

March   Newspaper stamp reduced.
June   London Working Men's Association formed.

1837

January   East London Democratic Association formed.
February   London Working Men's Association holds its first public meeting.
Petition to House of Commons adopted.
April   Strike of the Glasgow Cotton-Spinners.
Birmingham Political Union revived.
July   General election. Defeat of many Radical MPs.
November   South Lancashire Anti-Poor Law Association established.

1838

Political unions established.

April	Great Northern Union formed at Leeds.
May	People's Charter published in London.

National Petition published in Birmingham.

Mass meeting in Glasgow attended by representatives from Birmingham Political Union and London Working Men's Association.

June	Northern Political Union formed at Newcastle.
August	Great Birmingham rally.
September	Kersal Moor meeting, Manchester.

1839

February	General Convention of the Industrious Classes meets in London.
March	Anti-Corn Law League.
May	Convention moves to Birmingham.

Large demonstrations at Newcastle Town Moor, Peep Green in West Riding and Kersal Moor.

July	Bull Ring riots in Birmingham and arrest of Lovett and others.

Convention returns to London.

House of Commons rejects the first National Petition by 235 votes to 46.

Troubles in the North-East.

August	Rural Police Bill passed.

'Sacred Month' demonstrations.

September	Convention dissolved.
November	Newport rising.
Winter and spring	Chartist arrests.

1840

January	Abortive Sheffield and Bradford risings.
February–March	Chartist trials.
March	Scottish Christian Chartist movement becomes popular.
April	Northern Political Union reorganised in Newcastle.
March–April	Delegates meet in Manchester and Nottingham.
July	Chartist conference in Manchester.

National Charter Association established.

Autumn	Attempts made to create Chartist–Radical alliance in Leeds.

1841

Winter and spring	Teetotal Chartist societies established.
February	National Delegate Meeting at Manchester.
April	National Association of the United Kingdom for Promoting the Political and Social Improvement of the People established.
	O'Connor's attack on Knowledge, Christian and Temperance Chartism.
May	Petition Convention.
	Petition defeated in Parliament.
August	General election won by Sir Robert Peel and the Tories.

1842

April	Complete Suffrage Union Conference at Birmingham.
	Chartist Convention in London.
May	House of Commons rejects the second National Petition by 287 votes to 49.
August–September	Industrial unrest.
5 August	Strike begins at Stalybridge.
12 August	Conference of trade delegates in Manchester resolves to remain on strike until the Charter is law of the land.
15 August	Great Delegate Conference in Manchester.
16 August	Commemoration of 'Peterloo'.
	Turn-outs spread to Yorkshire.
20 August	Resolve of Manchester trade delegates begins to falter.
	Arrests begin.

1843

March	Trial of O'Connor and the other Chartists.
September	Chartist Convention in Birmingham, where land reform is accepted.
	Chartist Executive moves to London.
October	Harney becomes sub-editor of the *Northern Star*.

1844

April Chartist Convention in Manchester.

1845

April Chartist Convention in London.
Chartist Land Co-operative Society formed.
Autumn National Association of United Trades formed.
September Society of Fraternal Democrats established.
December Manchester Conference on the Land Plan.

1846

February Rising in Cracow, Poland.
June Repeal of the Corn Laws.
December Birmingham Conference on the Land Plan.

1847

May Ten Hours Factory Bill passed.
O'Connorville opened.
July General election won by Lord John Russell and the Whigs.
O'Connor elected at Nottingham.

1848

February Revolution in France.
April Chartist Convention in London.
Kennington Common demonstration.
Third National Petition ridiculed in Parliament.
Summer Chartist disturbances and arrests.
August Publication of Reports of the Select Committee of the House of Commons on the Land Company.

1849

June Reform motion defeated in House of Commons by 286 votes to 82.
December Chartist delegate conference in London.

1850

January Harney and the London Democrats assume leadership of the Chartist Executive.
June Harney's *Red Republican* published.
July Ernest Jones released from prison.

1851

January	Chartist Convention in Manchester.
February	Bill to dissolve the National Land Company.
March	Chartist Conference in London.
May	Ernest Jones's *Notes to the People* published.

1852

April	Harney buys the *Northern Star*.
	Ernest Jones launches the *People's Paper*.
	Chartist Convention in Manchester.

1853

Spring and summer	Brief revival of the Chartist movement.

1854

March	Labour parliament meets at Manchester.
	Britain enters the Crimean War.

1856

Spring	Chartist localities show new vigour.
July	Frost returns from exile.
	Death of O'Connor.

1858

February	Last national Chartist Convention.

Appendix: The Charter of 1837

Petition agreed to at the 'Crown and Anchor' meeting, 28 February 1837

To the Honourable the Commons of Great Britain and Ireland. The Petition of the undersigned Members of the Working Men's Association and others sheweth:

That the only rational use of the institutions and laws of society is justly to protect, encourage, and support all that can be made to contribute to the happiness of all the people.

That, as the object to be obtained is mutual benefit, so ought the enactment of laws to be by mutual consent.

That obedience to laws can only be justly enforced on the certainty that those who are called on to obey them have had, either personally or by their representatives, the power to enact, amend, or repeal them.

That all those who are excluded from this share of political power are not justly included within the operation of the laws; to them the laws are only despotic enactments, and the legislative assembly from whom they emanate can only be considered parties to an unholy compact, devising plans and schemes for taxing and subjecting the many.

That the universal political right of every human being is superior and stands apart from all customs, forms, or ancient usage; a fundamental right not in the power of man to confer; or justly to deprive him of.

That to take away this sacred right from the person and to vest it in property, is a wilful perversion of justice and common sense, as the creation and security of property are the consequences of society – the great object of which is human happiness.

That any constitution or code of laws, formed in violation of men's political and social rights, are not rendered sacred by time nor sanctified by custom.

That the ignorance which originated, or permits their operation, forms no excuse for perpetuating the injustice; nor can aught but force or fraud sustain them, when any considerable number of the people perceive and feel their degradation.

That the intent and object of your petitioners are to present such facts before your Honourable House as will serve to convince you and the country at large that you do not represent the people of these realms; and to appeal to your sense of right and justice as well as to every principle of honour, for directly making such legislative enactments as shall cause the mass of the people to be represented; with the view of securing the greatest amount of happiness to all classes of society. Your Petitioners find, by returns ordered by your Honourable House, that the whole people of Great Britain and Ireland are about 24 millions, and that the males above 21 years of age are 6,023,752, who, in the opinion of your petitioners, are justly entitled to the elective right.

That according to S. Wortley's return (ordered by your Honourable House) the number of registered electors, who have the power to vote for members of Parliament, are only 839,519, and of this number only 8½ in 12 give their votes.

That on an analysis of the constituency of the United Kingdom, your petitioners find that 331 members (being a majority of your Honourable House) are returned by one hundred and fifty-one thousand four hundred and ninety-two registered electors!

That comparing the whole of the male population above the age of 21 with the 151,492 electors, it appears that 1-40 of them, or 1-160 of the entire population, have the power of passing all the laws in your Honourable House.

And your petitioners further find on investigation, that this majority of 331 members are composed of 163 Tories or Conservatives, 134 Whigs and Liberals, and only 34 who call themselves Radicals; and out of this limited number it is questionable whether 10 can be found who are truly the representatives of the wants and wishes of the producing classes.

Your petitioners also find that 15 members of your Honourable House are returned by electors under 200; 55 under 300; 99 under 400; 121 under 500; 150 under 600; 196 under 700; 214 under 800; 240 under 900; and 256 under 1,000; and that many of these constituencies are divided between two members.

They also find that your Honourable House, which is said to be exclusively the people's or the Commons House, contains two hundred and five persons who are immediately or remotely related to the Peers of the Realm.

Also that your Honourable House contains 1 marquess, 7 earls, 19 viscounts, 32 lords, 25 right honourables, 52 honourables, 63 baronets, 13 knights, 3 admirals, 7 lord-lieutenants, 42 deputy and vice-lieutenants, 1 general, 5 lieutenant-generals, 9 major-generals, 32 colonels, 33 lieutenant-colonels, 10 majors, 49 captains in army and navy, 10 lieutenants, 2 cornets, 58 barristers, 3 solicitors, 40 bankers, 33 East India proprietors, 13 West India proprietors, 52 place-men, 114 patrons of church livings having the patronage of 274 livings between them; the names of whom your petitioners can furnish at the request of your Honourable House.

Your petitioners therefore respectfully submit to your Honourable House that these facts afford abundant proofs that you do not represent the numbers or the interests of the millions; but that the persons composing it have interests for the most part foreign or directly opposed to the true interests of the great body of the people. That perceiving the tremendous power you possess over the lives, liberty and labour of the unrepresented millions – perceiving the military and civil forces at your command – the revenue at your disposal – the relief of the poor in your hands – the public press in your power, by enactments expressly excluding the working classes alone moreover, the power of delegating to others the whole control of the monetary arrangements of the Kingdom, by which the labouring classes may be silently plundered or suddenly suspended from employment – seeing all these elements of power wielded by your Honourable House as at present constituted, and fearing the consequences that may result if a thorough reform is not speedily had recourse to, your petitioners earnestly pray your Honourable House to enact the following as the law of these realms, with such other essential details as your Honourable House shall deem necessary:-

A LAW FOR EQUALLY REPRESENTING THE PEOPLE OF GREAT BRITAIN AND IRELAND

Equal Representation
That the United Kingdom be divided into 200 electoral districts; dividing, as nearly as possible, an equal number of inhabitants; and that each district do send a representative to Parliament.

Universal Suffrage
That every person producing proof of his being 21 years of age, to the clerk of the parish in which he has resided six months, shall be entitled to have his name registered as a voter. That the time for registering in each year be from the 1st of January to the 1st of March.

Annual Parliaments

That a general election do take place on the 24th of June in each year, and that each vacancy be filled up a fortnight after it occurs. That the hours for voting be from six o'clock in the morning till six o'clock in the evening.

No Property Qualifications

That there shall be no property qualification for members; but on a requisition, signed by 200 voters, in favour of any candidate being presented to the clerk of the parish in which they reside, such candidate shall be put in nomination. And the list of all the candidates nominated throughout the district shall be stuck on the church door in every parish, to enable voters to judge of their qualification.

Vote by Ballot

That each voter must vote in the parish in which he resides. That each parish provide as many balloting boxes as there are candidates proposed in the district; and that a temporary place be fitted up in each parish church for the purpose of secret voting. And, on the day of election, as each voter passes orderly on to the ballot, he shall have given to him, by the officer in attendance, a balloting ball, which he shall drop into the box of his favourite candidate. At the close of the day the votes shall be counted, by the proper officers, and the numbers stuck on the church doors. The following day the clerk of the district and two examiners shall collect the votes of all the parishes throughout the district, and cause the name of the successful candidate to be posted in every parish of the district.

Sittings and Payments to Members

That the members do take their seats in Parliament on the first Monday in October next after their election, and continue their sittings every day (Sundays excepted) till the business of the sitting is terminated, but not later than the 1st of September. They shall meet every day (during the Session) for business at 10 o'clock in the morning, and adjourn at 4. And every member shall be paid quarterly out of the public treasury £400 a year. That all electoral officers shall be elected by universal suffrage.

By passing the foregoing as the law of the land, you will confer a great blessing on the people of England; and your petitioners, as in duty bound, will ever pray.

Notes

Chapter 1 The makings of a movement

1. Hopkins, E., *A Social History of the English Working Class 1815–1945*, Hodder and Stoughton, 1992, p. 18.
2. Brown, R. and Daniels, C., *Documents and Debates: The Chartists*, Macmillan, 1984, p. 18.
3. Hopkins, op. cit., p. 4.
4. Hopkins, op. cit., p. 9.
5. Quoted in Brown and Daniels, op. cit., p. 23.
6. Thompson, E.P., *The Making of the English Working Class*, Pantheon, 1964, p. 17.
7. Quoted by West, J. , *A History of the Chartist Movement*, Constable, 1920, p. 33.
8. Quoted by Rothstein, T., *From Chartism to Labourism*, Martin Lawrence, 1929, p. 33.
9. Ibid., p. 42.
10. Mill, J.S., *Considerations on Representative Government*, Collected Works XIX, Routledge and Kegan Paul, 1977, ch. 8, p. 478.
11. Quoted in Brown and Daniels, op. cit., pp. 27–8.

Chapter 2 The Newport rising: 1839

1. Thompson, D., *The Early Chartists*, Macmillan, 1971, p. 92.
2. Ibid., p. 206.
3. Ibid., p. 216.
4. Ward, J.T., *Chartism*, B.T. Batsford, 1973, p. 139.
5. Thompson, D., *The Early Chartists*, Wildwood House, 1984, p. 72.
6. Thompson, *The Early Chartists*, Macmillan, p. 237.
7. Jones, D., *The Last Rising*, Clarendon Press, 1985, p. 205.

Chapter 3 The first general strike: 1842

1. Quoted by Read, D., 'Chartism in Manchester', in Briggs, A. (ed.), *Chartist Studies*, Macmillan, 1965, p. 29.
2. Jenkins, M., *The General Strike of 1842*, Lawrence and Wishart, 1980, p. 48.
3. Engels, F., *The Condition of the Working Class in England*, Granada, 1979, p. 96.
4. Quoted by Read, op. cit., p. 32.
5. Brown, R., and Daniels, C., *Documents and Debates: The Chartists*, Macmillan, 1984, p. 85.
6. Ibid., pp. 89–90.
7. Schwartzkopf, J., *Women in the Chartist Movement*, Macmillan, 1991, p. 98.
8. Jenkins, op. cit., p. 15l.
9. Jenkins, op. cit., p. 154.
10. Quoted by Mather, in Briggs, op. cit., p. 389.
11. Engels, op. cit., p. 304.

Chapter 4 The years of drift: 1842–1848

1. Brown, R., and Daniels, C., *Documents and Debates: The Chartists*, Macmillan, 1984, p. 112.
2. Jones, D., *Chartism and the Chartists*, Penguin, 1975, p. 131.
3. Royle, E., *Chartism*, Longman, 1991, p. 119.
4. Saville, J., Introduction to Gammage, R.C., *History of the Chartist Movement 1837–54*, Cass, 1969, p. 58.
5. Jones, op. cit., p. 114.
6. Wright, D.G., *The Chartist Risings in Bradford*, Bradford, Libraries and Information Service, 1987, p. 5.
7. Jones, op. cit., p. 115.
8. Marx, K., 'Economic and Philosophical Manuscripts' in McLellan, D. (ed.), *Karl Marx Selected Writings*, Oxford, 1987, p. 80.
9. Jones, op. cit., p. 116.
10. West, J., *A History of the Chartist Movement*, Butler and Tanner, 1920, p. 169.
11. Place, F., *Improvement of the Working People*, BM Place Collection, V 01 IC, p. 225.
12. Harrison, B., 'Teetotal Chartism', *History*, no. 58, 1973, p. 215.
13. Ibid., p. 194.
14. West, op. cit., p. 153.
15. Jones, op. cit., p. 45.
16. Jones, op. cit., p. 52.

17. Jones, D., op. cit., p. 43.
18. *Northern Star*, 10 October 1840, quoted by Mather in *Chartism and Society: An Anthology of Documents*, Bell and Hyman, 1980, pp. 105–6.
19. Read, D., 'Chartism in Manchester', in Briggs, A. (ed.), *Chartist Studies*, Macmillan, 1965, pp. 31–2.
20. O'Higgins, R., *Past and Present*, no. 20, 1961, p. 86.
21. Thompson, D., 'Ireland and the Irish in English Radicalism before 1850' in Epstein, J., and Thompson, D. (eds.), *The Chartist Experience: Studies in Working-Class Radicalism and Culture, 1830–60*, Macmillan, 1982, p. 141.
22. Ibid., p. 142.
23. Haraszti, E.H., *Chartism*, Akademiai Kiado, Budapest, 1978, p. 246.
24. Thompson, D., *The Chartists*, Wildwood, 1984, p. 132.
25. Challinor, R., 'P.M. McDouall and Physical Force Chartism', *International Socialism Journal*, no. 12.
26. Thompson, D., *Chartist Experience*, op. cit., p. 146.
27. Alexander, P., *Racism, Resistance and Revolution*, Bookmarks, 1987, p. 141.
28. Cliff, T., *Rosa Luxemburg*, Bookmarks, 1983, pp. 36–7.

Chapter 5 The final confrontation: 1848

1. Saville, J., *1848: The British State and the Chartist Movement*, Cambridge University Press, 1987, pp. 34–5.
2. Weisser, H., *Challenge and Response in England in 1848*, University Press of America, 1983, p. 29.
3. Schoyen, A.R., *The Chartist Challenge: A Portrait of George Julian Harney*, Heinemann, 1958, p. 157.
4. Weisser, op. cit., p. 13.
5. Royle, E., *Chartism*, Longman, 1991, p. 124.
6. Brown, R., and Daniels, C., *Documents and Debates: The Chartists*, Macmillan, 1984, p. 124.
7. Ibid., pp. 126–7.
8. West, J., *A History of the Chartist Movement*, Butler and Tanner, 1920, p. 245.
9. Weisser, op. cit., p. 57.
10. Saville, op. cit., p. 105.
11. Saville, J., *Ernest Jones: Chartist*, Lawrence and Wishart, 1952, p. 98.
12. Ibid., p. 105.
13. West, op. cit., p. 246.

14. Saville, op. cit., p. 110.
15. Weisser, op. cit., p. 79.
16. Cole, G.D.H., *Chartist Portraits*, Macmillan, 1965, pp. 348–9.

Chapter 6 Leaders and socialists

1. Epstein, J., *The Lion of Freedom: Feargus O'Connor and the Chartist Movement 1832–42*, Croom Helm, 1982, p. 63.
2. Read, D., and Glasgow, E., *Feargus O'Connor – Irishman and Chartist*, Arnold, 1961.
3. Epstein, op. cit., p. 70.
4. Epstein, op. cit., p. 71.
5. Epstein, op. cit., p. 70.
6. Plummer, A., *Bronterre: A Political Biography of Bronterre O'Brien*, George Allen and Unwin, 1971, p. 61.
7. Saville, J., *Ernest Jones: Chartist*, Lawrence and Wishart, 1952, p. 37.
8. Ibid., p. 41.
9. Schoyen, A.R., *The Chartist Challenge: A Portrait of George Julian Harney*, Heinemann, 1958, p. 156.
10. Ibid., p. 202.

Chapter 7 Marxism and the Chartist movement

1. Ward, J.T., *Chartism*, B.T. Batsford, 1973, p. 239.
2. Engels, F., 'On England', *Marx/Engels Collected Works* (MECW), Vol. 11, pp. 200–1.
3. Engels, F., 'Socialism: utopian and scientific', MECW, Vol. 24, p. 304.
4. Engels, F., 'Letters from London', MECW, Vol. 3, pp. 379–80.
5. Marx, K. and Engels, F., 'Fictitious splits in the International', MECW, Vol. 23, p. 106.
6. Engels, F. to Marx, K., 'Letters', MECW, Vol. 39, p. 68.
7. Marx, K., 'The Chartists', MECW, Vol. 11, pp. 335–6.
8. Marx, K., 'The Association for Administrative Reform', MECW, Vol. 14, p. 243.
9. Marx, K., and Engels, F., 'The German ideology', MECW, Vol. 5, p. 217.
10. Engels, F., 'The condition of the working class of England in 1844', MECW, Vol. 3, p. 450.
11. Marx, K., 'The revolutionary movement', MECW, Vol. 8, pp. 214–15.
12. Marx, K., 'On Poland', MECW, Vol. 6, p. 389.

General index

Index of places